Studies in World History

DR. JAMES STOBAUGH

STORY RELIGION GEOGRAPHY

HISTORY RELIGION

ONOMICS GOVERNMENT

GEOGRAPHY ECONOMICS GOVERNMENT

Vol. 2
The New World
to the Modern Age
{1500 A.D. to 1900 A.D}.

TEACHER GUIDE

Includes: Answer Keys

Daily Calendar

Daily Discussion Questions

Weekly Exams

First printing: March 2014

Master Books®, P.O. Box 726, Green Forest, AR 72638

Master Books® is a division of the New Leaf Publishing Group, Inc.

ISBN: 978-0-89051-792-5

Unless otherwise noted, Scripture quotations are from the New King James Version of the Bible.

Printed in the United States of America

Please visit our website for other great titles:

www.masterbooks.net

For information regarding author interviews,

please contact the publicity department at (870) 438-5288

Master Books®
A Division of New Leaf Publishing Group
www.masterbooks.net

Where Creation Inspires Education

Since 1975, Master Books has been providing educational resources based on a biblical worldview to students of all ages. At the heart of these resources is our firm belief in a literal six-day creation, a young earth, the global Flood as revealed in Genesis 1–11, and other vital evidence to help build a critical foundation of scriptural authority for everyone. By equipping students with biblical truths and their key connection to the world of science and history, it is our hope they will be able to defend their faith in a skeptical, fallen world.

If the foundations are destroyed, what can the righteous do?
Psalm 11:3; NKJV

As the largest publisher of creation science materials in the world, Master Books is honored to partner with our authors and educators, including:

Ken Ham of Answers in Genesis

Dr. John Morris and Dr. Jason Lisle of the Institute for Creation Research

Dr. Donald DeYoung and Michael Oard of the Creation Research Society

Dr. James Stobaugh, John Hudson Tiner, Rick and Marilyn Boyer, Dr. Tom DeRosa, Todd Friel, Israel Wayne and so many more!

Whether a preschool learner or a scholar seeking an advanced degree, we offer a wonderful selection of award-winning resources for all ages and educational levels.

But sanctify the Lord God in your hearts, and always be ready
to give a defense to everyone who asks you a reason for the hope
that is in you, with meekness and fear.
1 Peter 3:15; NKJV

Permission to Copy

Lessons for a 34-week course!

Overview: This *Studies in World History Volume 2 Teacher Guide* contains materials for use with *Studies in World History Volume 2*. Materials are organized by book in the following sections:

📇	Study guide worksheets
E	Exams
🔑	Answer Key

Features: Each suggested weekly schedule has five easy-to-manage lessons that combine reading, worksheets, and optional exams. Worksheets and exams are perforated and three-hole punched – materials are easy to tear out, hand out, grade, and store. You are encouraged to adjust the schedule and materials needed to best work within your educational program.

Workflow: Students will read the pages in their book and then complete each section of the Teacher Guide. Exams are given at regular intervals with space to record each grade. If used with younger students, they may be given the option of taking open-book exams.

Lesson Scheduling: Space is given for assignment dates. There is flexibility in scheduling. For example, the parent may opt for a M, W, F schedule, rather than a M-F schedule. Each week listed has five days but due to vacations the school work week may not be M-F. Adapt the days to your school schedule. As the student completes each assignment, he/she should put an "X" in the box.

🕐	Approximately 20 to 30 minutes per lesson, five days a week
🔑	Includes answer keys for worksheets and exams
📇	Worksheets for each section
🔁	Exams are included to help reinforce learning and provide assessment opportunities
📄	Designed for grades 7 to 9 in a one-year course to earn 1 history credit

Dr. James Stobaugh was a Merrill Fellow at Harvard and holds degrees from Vanderbilt and Rutgers universities, and Princeton and Gordon-Conwell seminaries. An experienced teacher, he is a recognized leader in homeschooling and has published numerous books for students and teachers, including a high school history series (American, British, and World), as well as a companion high school literature series. He and his wife Karen have homeschooled their four children since 1985.

Contents

Introduction

The junior high student will see history come to life no matter what his or her pace or ability. Developed by Dr. James Stobaugh, these courses grow in difficulty with each year, preparing students for high school work. This is a comprehensive examination of history, geography, economics, and government systems. This educational set equips students to learn from a starting point of God's creation of the world and move forward with a solid biblically based worldview. Volume 2 covers the clash of cultures, Europe and the Renaissance, Reformation, revolutions, and more.

How this course has been developed:

1. Chapters: This course has 34 chapters (representing 34 weeks of study).

2. Lessons: Each chapter has five lessons, taking approximately 20 to 30 minutes each. There is a short reading followed by discussion questions. Some questions require a specific answer from the text, while others are more open ended, leading students to think "outside the box."

3. Weekly exams: This Teacher Guide includes two optional exams for each chapter.

4. Student responsibility: Responsibility to complete this course is on the student. Students are to complete the readings every day, handing their responses in to a parent or teacher for evaluation. This course was designed for students to practice independent learning.

5. Grading: Students turn in assignments to a parent or teacher for grading.

Throughout the student text are the following components:

1. First thoughts: Background on the historical period.

2. Discussion questions: Questions based generally on Bloom's Taxonomy.

3. Concepts: Terms, concepts, and theories to be learned that are bolded for emphasis. Most are listed on the first page of the chapter and in the glossary.

4. History makers: A person(s) who clearly changed the course of history.

5. Historical debate: An examination of historical theories surrounding a period or topic.

First Semester Suggested Daily Schedule

Date	Day	Assignment	Due Date	✓	Grade
		First Semester — First Quarter			

Chapter 1: Medieval Europe: Technology Triumphs
A century before Columbus sailed, Europeans were probing the coast of Africa and eventually reached the East Indies going east to China long before Columbus departed, sure that he could do the same thing going west.

	Day	Assignment	Due Date	✓	Grade
	Day 1	Read **Lesson 1 — End of the Middle Ages** Student Book (SB) Answer Discussion Question Page 21 Lesson Planner (LP)			
	Day 2	Read **Lesson 2 — Viking Settlements in North America** (SB) Answer Discussion Question Page 22 (LP)			
Week 1	Day 3	Read **Lesson 3 — Portuguese: Influence of One Man . . .** (SB) Answer Discussion Question Page 23 (LP)			
	Day 4	Read **Lesson 4 — Economic: Private Investments** (SB) Answer Discussion Question Page 24 (LP)			
	Day 5	Read **Lesson 5 — Advances in Technology: The Caravel . . .** (SB) Answer Discussion Question Page 25 (LP) Optional **Lesson 1 Exam** 1 or 2 Page 227–228 (LP)			

Chapter 2: The Americas: On the Eve of Invasion
The same impulse that would drive humans to build a computer and go to the moon would first take mankind from Western Europe to the New World. What made this possible, partly, besides pathos, was the superior technology that Western Europe brought to the table.

	Day	Assignment	Due Date	✓	Grade
	Day 6	Read **Lesson 1 — On the Mountains of the Prairie** (SB) Answer Discussion Question Page 27 (LP)			
	Day 7	Read **Lesson 2 — Sociology: . . . Native American Societies** (SB) Answer Discussion Question Page 28 (LP)			
Week 2	Day 8	Read **Lesson 3 — Anthropology: Kinship** (SB) Answer Discussion Question Page 29 (LP)			
	Day 9	Read **Lesson 4 — Government: The Native American Chief** (SB) Answer Discussion Question Page 30 (LP)			
	Day 10	Read **Lesson 5 — Ethnocentricity** (SB) Answer Discussion Question Page 31 (LP) Optional **Lesson 2 Exam** 1 or 2 Page 229–230 (LP)			

Chapter 3: European Exploration: Technology Married to Idealism
The times were good in Europe in the early 1490s. There was prosperity everywhere, and the people were optimistic. They were more than ready to initiate, contribute to, and join in the Age of Exploration.

	Day	Assignment	Due Date	✓	Grade
	Day 11	Read **Lesson 1 — Cartography and Mapmaking** (SB) Answer Discussion Question Page 33 (LP)			
	Day 12	Read **Lesson 2 — The Search for the Northwest Passage** (SB) Answer Discussion Question Page 34 (LP)			
Week 3	Day 13	Read **Lesson 3 — Secondary Source (A fairly inaccurate . . .)** (SB) Answer Discussion Question Page 35 (LP)			
	Day 14	Read **Lesson 4 — The Limits of Secondary Sources** (SB) Answer Discussion Question Page 36 (LP)			
	Day 15	Read **Lesson 5 — Contributions to Geography** (SB) Answer Discussion Question Page 37 (LP) Optional **Lesson 3 Exam** 1 or 2 Page 231–232 (LP)			

Chapter 4: Clash of Cultures: Native Americans and the Europeans

As the world expanded, it created conflicts; a foreign people group, unrehearsed, invaded and, in this case, conquered another people. This tragic drama was to be played out from Jamestown to Anchorage for the next 400 years.

Date	Day	Assignment	Due Date	✓	Grade
Week 4	Day 16	Read **Lesson 1 — First Encounters** (SB) Answer Discussion Question Page 39 (LP)			
	Day 17	Read **Lesson 2 — Accommodation** (SB) Answer Discussion Question Page 40 (LP)			
	Day 18	Read **Lesson 3 — Nation Building** (SB) Answer Discussion Question Page 41 (LP)			
	Day 19	Read **Lesson 4 — Native Americans and European ...** (SB) Answer Discussion Question Page 42 (LP)			
	Day 20	Read **Lesson 5 — Lewis Wetzel: A Case Study** (SB) Answer Discussion Question Page 43 (LP) Optional **Lesson 4 Exam** 1 or 2 Page 233–234 (LP)			

Chapter 5: Meanwhile in Europe: Crisis of Celebration

Europe had emerged from the Middle Ages full of vigor, full of budding prosperity, but disorientated. It was not the first, and would not be the last, civilization that was as disoriented by victory as others were by defeat. This was in fact a crisis of celebration.

Date	Day	Assignment	Due Date	✓	Grade
Week 5	Day 21	Read **Lesson 1 — Russia in the 17th Century** (SB) Answer Discussion Question Page 45 (LP)			
	Day 22	Read **Lesson 2 — The Swedish Empire: Nationalist Revolt** (SB) Answer Discussion Question Page 46 (LP)			
	Day 23	Read **Lesson 3 — Economics: Commercialized Surpluses** (SB) Answer Discussion Question Page 47 (LP)			
	Day 24	Read **Lesson 4 — Sociology: Urbanization** (SB) Answer Discussion Question Page 48 (LP)			
	Day 25	Read **Lesson 5 — International Warfare** (SB) Answer Discussion Question Page 49 (LP) Optional **Lesson 5 Exam** 1 or 2 Page 235–236 (LP)			

Chapter 6: The Renaissance: The Problem of Progress

Europeans would continue the dance of death until one or the other philosophies would win or lose. Changes were coming, and they would sweep through Europe like a fire.

Date	Day	Assignment	Due Date	✓	Grade
Week 6	Day 26	Read **Lesson 1 — The World Awoke as From Sleep** (SB) Answer Discussion Question Page 51 (LP)			
	Day 27	Read **Lesson 2 — The Italian Renaissance** (SB) Answer Discussion Question Page 52 (LP)			
	Day 28	Read **Lesson 3 — Italian City States** (SB) Answer Discussion Question Page 53 (LP)			
	Day 29	Read **Lesson 4 — The Importance of Printing** (SB) Answer Discussion Question Page 54 (LP)			
	Day 30	Read **Lesson 5 — Erasmus and Northern Humanism** (SB) Answer Discussion Question Page 55 (LP) Optional **Lesson 6 Exam** 1 or 2 Page 237–238 (LP)			

Date	Day	Assignment	Due Date	✓	Grade

Chapter 7: Art: The Refinement of the Artificial

The definition of beauty was on a slippery slope that began here. It was one thing for beauty to be a sensual Madonna painted in a garden. It was another thing for the United States government, in the 1980s, to fund an art project that featured a crucifix in a jar of human urine. As early as 1600, the world of art was headed to a world of woes.

Date	Day	Assignment	Due Date	✓	Grade
Week 7	Day 31	Read **Lesson 1 — Art Is Everywhere** (SB) Answer Discussion Question Page 57 (LP)			
	Day 32	Read **Lesson 2 — Pre-Renaissance Art** (SB) Answer Discussion Question Page 58 (LP)			
	Day 33	Read **Lesson 3 — Michelangelo, da Vinci, and Raphael** (SB) Answer Discussion Question Page 59 (LP)			
	Day 34	Read **Lesson 4 — Baroque Era** (SB) Answer Discussion Question Page 60 (LP)			
	Day 35	Read **Lesson 5 — Secondary Source** (SB) Answer Discussion Question Page 61 (LP) Optional **Lesson 7 Exam** 1 or 2 Page 239–240 (LP)			

Chapter 8: The Reformation: Grace Burst Forth

There was never a war, never a revolution, that surpassed this ubiquitous of cultural revolutions begun by a gentle monk nailing 95 theses on a door in Wittenberg, Germany, in the 16th century.

Date	Day	Assignment	Due Date	✓	Grade
Week 8	Day 36	Read **Lesson 1 — The Causes** (SB) Answer Discussion Question Page 63 (LP)			
	Day 37	Read **Lesson 2 — Grace** (SB) Answer Discussion Question Page 64 (LP)			
	Day 38	Read **Lesson 3 — A Revolution Means War** (SB) Answer Discussion Question Page 65 (LP)			
	Day 39	Read **Lesson 4 — The Roman Catholic Counterreformation** (SB) Answer Discussion Question Page 66 (LP)			
	Day 40	Read **Lesson 5 — Counterreformation Primary Source** (SB) Answer Discussion Question Page 67 (LP) Optional **Lesson 8 Exam** 1 or 2 Page 241–242 (LP)			

Chapter 9: Philosophy: The Nature of Government

Government was to be the way God ordained mankind to sustain and to limit other men. It was not to be a trivial or easy thing to maintain in the years to come. Justice, especially, was an elusive goal.

Date	Day	Assignment	Due Date	✓	Grade
Week 9	Day 41	Read **Lesson 1 — Essay** (SB) Answer Discussion Question Page 69 (LP)			
	Day 42	Read **Lesson 2 — Constitutional Governments** (SB) Answer Discussion Question Page 70 (LP)			
	Day 43	Read **Lesson 3 — Absolutism** (SB) Answer Discussion Question Page 71 (LP)			
	Day 44	Read **Lesson 4 — Thomas Hobbes, Philosopher** (SB) Answer Discussion Question Page 72 (LP)			
	Day 45	Read **Lesson 5 — Moral Absolutism** (SB) Answer Discussion Question Page 73 (LP) Optional **Lesson 9 Exam** 1 or 2 Page 243–244 (LP)			

First Semester — Second Quarter

Chapter 10: Religion and Science: The Scientific Revolution

Like Victor Frankenstein in Mary Shelley's novel, the world was to produce "monsters" that both blessed and cursed their disciples. Science was a more popular faith expression than religion, Roman Catholic or Protestant, could provide. The world dated science in the 18th century; it married science in the 19th.

Week 1	Day 46	Read **Lesson 1 — Science and Religion** (SB) Answer Discussion Question Page 75 (LP)			
	Day 47	Read **Lesson 2 — Inductive and Deductive Reasoning** (SB) Answer Discussion Question Page 76 (LP)			
	Day 48	Read **Lesson 3 — The Day the Sun Stood Still** (SB) Answer Discussion Question Page 77 (LP)			
	Day 49	Read **Lesson 4 — Imperialist Science** (SB) Answer Discussion Question Page 78 (LP)			
	Day 50	Read **Lesson 5 — Science Gone too Far** (SB) Answer Discussion Question Page 79 (LP) Optional **Lesson 10 Exam** 1 or 2 Page 245–246 (LP)			

Chapter 11: Chattel Slavery: The Long Ordeal

How tragic, how ironic, that the most profitable institution in the New World was not agriculture or industry or even mining gold. It was slavery.

Week 2	Day 51	Read **Lesson 1 — Slavery in the Ancient World** (SB) Answer Discussion Question Page 81 (LP)			
	Day 52	Read **Lesson 2 — Slavery in Africa** (SB) Answer Discussion Question Page 82 (LP)			
	Day 53	Read **Lesson 3 — The Slave Trade** (SB) Answer Discussion Question Page 83 (LP)			
	Day 54	Read **Lesson 4 — The Atlantic Slave Trade** (SB) Answer Discussion Question Page 84 (LP)			
	Day 55	Read **Lesson 5 — The Middle Passage** (SB) Answer Discussion Question Page 85 (LP) Optional **Lesson 11 Exam** 1 or 2 Page 247–248 (LP)			

Chapter 12: Slavery in the New World: A Peculiar Institution

What makes the story more horrible is that slavery began, not in the ports of West Africa, but in sub-Saharan African villages and North African Islamic trading posts. Slavery in the New World, then, was enabled by slavery in the Old World, in Africa itself. It existed then; it exists now.

Week 3	Day 56	Read **Lesson 1 — Slavery in the New World** (SB) Answer Discussion Question Page 87 (LP)			
	Day 57	Read **Lesson 2 — Comparing Old World and New World . . .** (SB) Answer Discussion Question Page 88 (LP)			
	Day 58	Read **Lesson 3 — A Culture Under Stress: Slave Culture** (SB) Answer Discussion Question Page 89 (LP)			
	Day 59	Read **Lesson 4 — Slave Resistance** (SB) Answer Discussion Question Page 90 (LP)			
	Day 60	Read **Lesson 5 — Comparison of Slavery in the Americas** (SB) Answer Discussion Question Page 91 (LP) Optional **Lesson 12 Exam** 1 or 2 Page 249–250 (LP)			

Date	Day	Assignment	Due Date	✓	Grade

Chapter 13: Revolution: The Rise of Liberty

Revolution as a concept did not occur until the 18th century. There were uprisings, riots, but no rebellions. Revolution, then, was something very new. It would become the preferred choice of social radicals from now on.

Date	Day	Assignment	Due Date	✓	Grade
	Day 61	Read **Lesson 1 — Revolution in Rome** (SB) Answer Discussion Question Page 93 (LP)			
	Day 62	Read **Lesson 2 — Secondary Source** (SB) Answer Discussion Question Page 94 (LP)			
Week 4	Day 63	Read **Lesson 3 — The Jacobite Uprising of 1745** (SB) Answer Discussion Question Page 95 (LP)			
	Day 64	Read **Lesson 4 — American Revolution: The First Modern . . .** (SB) Answer Discussion Question Page 96 (LP)			
	Day 65	Read **Lesson 5 — The French Revolution: A Good Thing . . .** (SB) Answer Discussion Question Page 97 (LP) Optional **Lesson 13 Exam** 1 or 2 Page 251–252 (LP)			

Chapter 14: Revivalism: God Sightings

In Europe new converts were born into the faith. In America they went to revivals too. A new pattern emerged in the 18th century that would transform Christianity: revivalism. It would remain the pattern at least until the 21st century.

Date	Day	Assignment	Due Date	✓	Grade
	Day 66	Read **Lesson 1 — A 100-Year Prayer Meeting** (SB) Answer Discussion Question Page 99 (LP)			
	Day 67	Read **Lesson 2 — The Anabaptists** (SB) Answer Discussion Question Page 100 (LP)			
Week 5	Day 68	Read **Lesson 3 — The Puritans: A Premodern Christian State** (SB) Answer Discussion Question Page 101 (LP)			
	Day 69	Read **Lesson 4 — Historical Debate: The Great Awakening** (SB) Answer Discussion Question Page 102 (LP)			
	Day 70	Read **Lesson 5 — A Religious Movement Affects All Society** (SB) Answer Discussion Question Page 103 (LP) Optional **Lesson 14 Exam** 1 or 2 Page 253–254 (LP)			

Chapter 15: The Word: History of the English Bible

The King James Bible was spurned by all evangelicals until the 19th century yet, without a doubt, it became the most popular Bible in history.

Date	Day	Assignment	Due Date	✓	Grade
	Day 71	Read **Lesson 1 — Background** (SB) Answer Discussion Question Page 105 (LP)			
	Day 72	Read **Lesson 2 — Formation of the Canon** (SB) Answer Discussion Question Page 106 (LP)			
Week 6	Day 73	Read **Lesson 3 — English Bible History** (SB) Answer Discussion Question Page 107 (LP)			
	Day 74	Read **Lesson 4 — The King James Bible** (SB) Answer Discussion Question Page 108 (LP)			
	Day 75	Read **Lesson 5 — Essay: Secondary Source Opinion** (SB) Answer Discussion Question Page 109 (LP) Optional **Lesson 15 Exam** 1 or 2 Page 255–256 (LP)			

Chapter 16: Sociology: Prospering in a Hostile Culture

No civilization in the western hemisphere was founded with higher, fonder hopes than the Puritan civilization. It was a noble experiment. Notwithstanding jeremiads and soothsayers it has persevered in our government, in our culture, in our religion. Nothing has been more enduring in our kaleidoscopic nation.

	Day	Assignment		
	Day 76	Read **Lesson 1 — John Winthrop** (SB) Answer Discussion Question Page 111 (LP)		
	Day 77	Read **Lesson 2 — The New England Confederation . . .** (SB) Answer Discussion Question Page 112 (LP)		
Week 7	Day 78	Read **Lesson 3 — King Philip's War** (SB) Answer Discussion Question Page 113 (LP)		
	Day 79	Read **Lesson 4 — Edmund Andros** (SB) Answer Discussion Question Page 114 (LP)		
	Day 80	Read **Lesson 5 — Puritan Laws and Character** (SB) Answer Discussion Question Page 115 (LP) Optional **Lesson 16 Exam** 1 or 2 Page 257–258 (LP)		

Chapter 17: Primary Sources: Eighteenth Century

History is always about people — their dreams, fears, successes, joys, and failures. It was in the 18th century and would be forever.

	Day	Assignment		
	Day 81	Read **Lesson 1 — "A Soldier's Diary," by Robert Moses** (SB) Answer Discussion Question Page 117 (LP)		
	Day 82	Read **Lesson 2 — Accounts...of the Revival of Religion, 1743** (SB) Answer Discussion Question Page 118 (LP)		
Week 8	Day 83	Read **Lesson 3 — Immigration and Ethnic Diversity** (SB) Answer Discussion Question Page 119 (LP)		
	Day 84	Read **Lesson 4 — Fear of Slave Revolts** (SB) Answer Discussion Question Page 120 (LP)		
	Day 85	Read **Lesson 5 — The Diary of Mary Cooper** (SB) Answer Discussion Question Page 121 (LP) Optional **Lesson 17 Exam** 1 or 2 Page 259–260 (LP)		

Chapter 18: Founding Fathers: The Power of the Myth

Nations, civilizations have one or two, but usually no more, heroes and heroines who are revered as the progenitors of a nation. America, though, is a wealthy people with many more founding heroes who would be vilified, and by others, practically worshipped. But they were real, they were genuine heroes. And they walk among us today.

	Day	Assignment		
	Day 86	Read **Lesson 1 — John Adams (1735–1826)** (SB) Answer Discussion Question Page 123 (LP)		
	Day 87	Read **Lesson 2 — Samuel Adams (1722–1803)** (SB) Answer Discussion Question Page 124 (LP)		
Week 9	Day 88	Read **Lesson 3 — Benjamin Franklin (1706–1790)** (SB) Answer Discussion Question Page 125 (LP)		
	Day 89	Read **Lesson 4 — Alexander Hamilton (1755–1804)** (SB) Answer Discussion Question Page 126 (LP)		
	Day 90	Read **Lesson 5 — Secondary Source** (SB) Answer Discussion Question Page 127 (LP) Optional **Lesson 18 Exam** 1 or 2 Page 261–262 (LP)		
		Midterm Grade		

Second Semester Suggested Daily Schedule

Date	Day	Assignment	Due Date	✓	Grade
		Second Semester — Third Quarter			

Chapter 19: Eighteenth-Century Life: The Family

The American family underwent a radical change in the 19th century. Couples fell in love, and most would die in love. Many were horrified at the prospect. Before the detractors, however, could become comfortable with the idea, things would change. And not for the better. How ironical and tragic that this universal marital love would not last into the 20th century. By the beginning of the 20st century, over half of American marriages would end in divorce.

Date	Day	Assignment	Due Date	✓	Grade
Week 1	Day 91	Read **Lesson 1 — Childbirth in Early America** (SB) Answer Discussion Question Page 129 (LP)			
	Day 92	Read **Lesson 2 — Courtship in Early America** (SB) Answer Discussion Question Page 130 (LP)			
	Day 93	Read **Lesson 3 — Death in Early America** (SB) Answer Discussion Question Page 131 (LP)			
	Day 94	Read **Lesson 4 — Overview of Eighteenth-Century Art** (SB) Answer Discussion Question Page 132 (LP)			
	Day 95	Read **Lesson 5 — Secondary Source** (SB) Answer Discussion Question Page 133 (LP) Optional **Lesson 19 Exam** 1 or 2 Page 263–264 (LP)			

Chapter 20: Great Battles: The Eighteenth Century

How strange it was that humans determined the fate of their nations by warfare. Total war emerged in the 18th century, and it would stay with us. More and more battles would become wars, and wars would be battles. And millions would die.

Date	Day	Assignment	Due Date	✓	Grade
Week 2	Day 96	Read **Lesson 1 — Battle of Narva — 1700** (SB) Answer Discussion Question Page 135 (LP)			
	Day 97	Read **Lesson 2 — Battle of Blenheim — 1704** (SB) Answer Discussion Question Page 136 (LP)			
	Day 98	Read **Lesson 3 — Battle of Quebec...Plains of Abraham — 1759** (SB) Answer Discussion Question Page 137 (LP)			
	Day 99	Read **Lesson 4 — The Battle of Lexington and Concord — 1775** (SB) Answer Discussion Question Page 138 (LP)			
	Day 100	Read **Lesson 5 — The Battle of Hohenlinden — 1800** (SB) Answer Discussion Question Page 139 (LP) Optional **Lesson 20 Exam** 1 or 2 Page 265–266 (LP)			

Chapter 21: Eighteenth-Century Science: Uneasiness in Zion

Science ended the 18th century with an uneasy truce with itself. Some would say it was a conflict with religion. But it wasn't really. It was a crisis within science. It was a family feud. Science made claims for itself it could not keep, would not keep, did not really want to keep. The further science discovered knowledge, the more knowledge pointed to God. Still, in the 18th century science would lose its way. But not yet. Not until Charles Darwin.

Date	Day	Assignment	Due Date	✓	Grade
Week 3	Day 101	Read **Lesson 1 — Attacking History** (SB) Answer Discussion Question Page 141 (LP)			
	Day 102	Read **Lesson 2 — Overview** (SB) Answer Discussion Question Page 142 (LP)			
	Day 103	Read **Lesson 3 — Age of Enlightenment** (SB) Answer Discussion Question Page 143 (LP)			
	Day 104	Read **Lesson 4 — Joseph Priestley** (SB) Answer Discussion Question Page 144 (LP)			
	Day 105	Read **Lesson 5 — Friedrich Wilhelm (William) Herschel** (SB) Answer Discussion Question Page 145 (LP) Optional **Lesson 21 Exam** 1 or 2 Page 267–268 (LP)			

Chapter 22: Reflections of an Age: Eighteenth-Century Voices

To find what really happens in history, one has to look in dining rooms, not in boardrooms, churches, or war rooms. This was to be the pattern from now until forever.

	Day	Assignment			
Week 4	Day 106	Read **Lesson 1 — Olaudah Equiano** (SB) Answer Discussion Question Page 147 (LP)			
	Day 107	Read **Lesson 2 — Marquis de la Galissonière** (SB) Answer Discussion Question Page 148 (LP)			
	Day 108	Read **Lesson 3 — About the Duties of Husbands and Wives** (SB) Answer Discussion Question Page 149 (LP)			
	Day 109	Read **Lesson 4 — ...the Boston Latin Grammar School (1712)** (SB) Answer Discussion Question Page 150 (LP)			
	Day 110	Read **Lesson 5 — "The Watch on the Rhine," 1870** (SB) Answer Discussion Question Page 151 (LP) Optional **Lesson 22 Exam** 1 or 2 Page 269–270 (LP)			

Chapter 23: The Government: Articles of Confederation

How extraordinary that the United States of America was birthed in failure. Extraordinary. Perhaps, in light of what we face in the future, this can give us hope.

	Day	Assignment			
Week 5	Day 111	Read **Lesson 1 — Introduction** (SB) Answer Discussion Question Page 153 (LP)			
	Day 112	Read **Lesson 2 — Articles of Confederation** (SB) Answer Discussion Question Page 154 (LP)			
	Day 113	Read **Lesson 3 — The Tyranny of the Majority** (SB) Answer Discussion Question Page 155 (LP)			
	Day 114	Read **Lesson 4 — Shays' Rebellion** (SB) Answer Discussion Question Page 156 (LP)			
	Day 115	Read **Lesson 5 — Other Voices** (SB) Answer Discussion Question Page 157 (LP) Optional **Lesson 23 Exam** 1 or 2 Page 271–272 (LP)			

Chapter 24: Dissenting Voices: A Vocal Minority

Only England was as comfortable with dissenting voices as America. Perhaps that was the genius that assured the robustness of this Anglo-American civilization. It would draw us into the 21st century.

	Day	Assignment			
Week 6	Day 116	Read **Lesson 1 — New Ideas** (SB) Answer Discussion Question Page 159 (LP)			
	Day 117	Read **Lesson 2 — The First Antislavery Movement** (SB) Answer Discussion Question Page 160 (LP)			
	Day 118	Read **Lesson 3 — Racial Revolution** (SB) Answer Discussion Question Page 161 (LP)			
	Day 119	Read **Lesson 4 — Historical Debate** (SB) Answer Discussion Question Page 162 (LP)			
	Day 120	Read **Lesson 5 — The Knotty Problem of Immigration** (SB) Answer Discussion Question Page 163 (LP) Optional **Lesson 24 Exam** 1 or 2 Page 273–274 (LP)			

Date	Day	Assignment	Due Date	✓	Grade

Chapter 25: History Makers: Women of Faith

Christianity entered the 18th century divided among denominations for the first time in history, but in all places, with all confessions, it continued to transform history, not with its orthodoxy, but with its felicity and love.

Date	Day	Assignment	Due Date	✓	Grade
Week 7	Day 121	Read **Lesson 1 — Madame Guyon, Pacifist Prayer Warrior** (SB) Answer Discussion Question Page 165 (LP)			
	Day 122	Read **Lesson 2 — Phillis Wheatley, Slave Evangelist-Poet** (SB) Answer Discussion Question Page 166 (LP)			
	Day 123	Read **Lesson 3 — Christina Georgina Rossetti, A Woman Who Could Have Been Anything** (SB) Answer Discussion Question Page 167 (LP)			
	Day 124	Read **Lesson 4 — Hanna Whitall Smith, Holiness Advocate** (SB) Answer Discussion Question Page 168 (LP)			
	Day 125	Read **Lesson 5 — "A Gathered Inheritance"** (SB) Answer Discussion Question Page 169 (LP) Optional **Lesson 25 Exam** 1 or 2 Page 275–276 (LP)			

Chapter 26: Religion: Eighteenth-Century Musings

The voices of the West inevitably found power in rhetoric. The preservation of that rhetoric, the retention of its metaphors, was and will determine the health of those societies.

Date	Day	Assignment	Due Date	✓	Grade
Week 8	Day 126	Read **Lesson 1 — The Jefferson Bible** (SB) Answer Discussion Question Page 171 (LP)			
	Day 127	Read **Lesson 2 — David Hume, "An Enquiry Concerning . . . "** (SB) Answer Discussion Question Page 172 (LP)			
	Day 128	Read **Lesson 3 — Thomas Paine, Essays on Religion** (SB) Answer Discussion Question Page 173 (LP)			
	Day 129	Read **Lesson 4 — Joseph Addison, "Ode"** (SB) Answer Discussion Question Page 174 (LP)			
	Day 130	Read **Lesson 5 — John Wesley, "Letter to William Wilberforce"** (SB) Answer Discussion Question Page 175 (LP) Optional **Lesson 26 Exam** 1 or 2 Page 277–278 (LP)			

Chapter 27: Nineteenth-Century Europe: Revolution

If the 21st century seems to belong to Asia, the 19th century belonged to Europe. Never again would a region of the world so dominate world culture and politics.

Date	Day	Assignment	Due Date	✓	Grade
Week 9	Day 131	Read **Lesson 1 — Government: Back to Monarchies** (SB) Answer Discussion Question Page 177 (LP)			
	Day 132	Read **Lesson 2 — Russia — A Nation Out of Time, Out of Place** (SB) Answer Discussion Question Page 178 (LP)			
	Day 133	Read **Lesson 3 — Ottoman Empire** (SB) Answer Discussion Question Page 179 (LP)			
	Day 134	Read **Lesson 4 — Austria-Hungary** (SB) Answer Discussion Question Page 180 (LP)			
	Day 135	Read **Lesson 5 — England: Queen Victoria** (SB) Answer Discussion Question Page 181 (LP) Optional **Lesson 27 Exam** 1 or 2 Page 279–280 (LP)			

Second Semester — Fourth Quarter

Chapter 28: Nineteenth-Century Europe: A Peace That Failed

For two centuries, the failures of the Congress of Vienna and the emerging power of nationalism would determine the politics and sociologies of Europe.

Date	Day	Assignment	Due Date	✓	Grade
Week 1	Day 136	Read **Lesson 1 — The Unification of Germany** (SB) Answer Discussion Question Page 183 (LP)			
	Day 137	Read **Lesson 2 — Italy** (SB) Answer Discussion Question Page 184 (LP)			
	Day 138	Read **Lesson 3 — The Treaty of Vienna** (SB) Answer Discussion Question Page 185 (LP)			
	Day 139	Read **Lesson 4 — France, 1800–1850, Social Problems** (SB) Answer Discussion Question Page 186 (LP)			
	Day 140	Read **Lesson 5 — France, 1850–1914, Delusions of Grandeur** (SB) Answer Discussion Question Page 187 (LP) Optional **Lesson 28 Exam** 1 or 2 Page 281–282 (LP)			

Chapter 29: Nineteenth-Century American Life: Falling in Love

Families changed radically in the 19th century. That would be, of course, only the beginning of change. Today, as surely as families were changing in Cincinnati, Ohio, they are changing even more today.

Date	Day	Assignment	Due Date	✓	Grade
Week 2	Day 141	Read **Lesson 1 — Life in 19th-Century Cincinnati** (SB) Answer Discussion Question Page 189 (LP)			
	Day 142	Read **Lesson 2 — Historical Essay** (SB) Answer Discussion Question Page 190 (LP)			
	Day 143	Read **Lesson 3 — Three Types of Families** (SB) Answer Discussion Question Page 191 (LP)			
	Day 144	Read **Lesson 4 — Transcendentalism** (SB) Answer Discussion Question Page 192 (LP)			
	Day 145	Read **Lesson 5 — Free at Last** (SB) Answer Discussion Question Page 193 (LP) Optional **Lesson 29 Exam** 1 or 2 Page 283–284 (LP)			

Chapter 30: With Malice Toward None: The Power of Rhetoric

Today, the public relations expert, the speech writer create the rhetoric of the nation. This was not the rhetoric of the 19th century. It was birthed in valor, in sincerity, in intrepidness. The story of how we lost this gift is the story of what happens to our nation in the last two centuries.

Date	Day	Assignment	Due Date	✓	Grade
Week 3	Day 146	Read **Lesson 1 — James K. Polk** (SB) Answer Discussion Question Page 195 (LP)			
	Day 147	Read **Lesson 2 — Abraham Lincoln** (SB) Answer Discussion Question Page 196 (LP)			
	Day 148	Read **Lesson 3 — Otto von Bismarck** (SB) Answer Discussion Question Page 197 (LP)			
	Day 149	Read **Lesson 4 — Robert E. Lee's Farewell Address . . .** (SB) Answer Discussion Question Page 198 (LP)			
	Day 150	Read **Lesson 5 — Chief Joseph Speeches** (SB) Answer Discussion Question Page 199 (LP) Optional **Lesson 30 Exam** 1 or 2 Page 285–286 (LP)			

Date	Day	Assignment	Due Date	✓	Grade

Chapter 31: Asian Immigration: The Myth of the Melting Pot

From the beginning, America was never a melting pot. At least in the first generation, immigrants formed their own separate communities in the larger community called "America." This was to change during the second and third generation, but even today Americans love to think of themselves as Americans first, and our cultural identity second. The way we have treated our immigrants and how we treat them in the future will show how we see ourselves.

	Day	Assignment			
	Day 151	Read **Lesson 1 — Nakahama Manjiro** (SB) Answer Discussion Question Page 201 (LP)			
	Day 152	Read **Lesson 2 — Hawaii's Sugar Plantations** (SB) Answer Discussion Question Page 202 (LP)			
Week 4	Day 153	Read **Lesson 3 — Lee Chew** (SB) Answer Discussion Question Page 203 (LP)			
	Day 154	Read **Lesson 4 — Chinese Immigrants and the . . . Railroad** (SB) Answer Discussion Question Page 204 (LP)			
	Day 155	Read **Lesson 5 — A Chinese Merchant's Appeal to Congress** (SB) Answer Discussion Question Page 205 (LP) Optional **Lesson 31 Exam** 1 or 2 Page 287–288 (LP)			

Chapter 32: Nation Building: Social Policy Dissonance

Whether it is Baghdad or Berlin, nationalism remains a controversial international impulse. It builds nations and tears down worlds. Can one nation deposit its values and beliefs, however laudable, on another nation? Should this nation do this? These questions have not been answered satisfactorily.

	Day	Assignment			
	Day 156	Read **Lesson 1 — Nationalism** (SB) Answer Discussion Question Page 207 (LP)			
	Day 157	Read **Lesson 2 — Romanticism** (SB) Answer Discussion Question Page 208 (LP)			
Week 5	Day 158	Read **Lesson 3 — The Gothic Romance** (SB) Answer Discussion Question Page 209 (LP)			
	Day 159	Read **Lesson 4 — National Wars: The Franco-Prussian War** (SB) Answer Discussion Question Page 210 (LP)			
	Day 160	Read **Lesson 5 — 19th-Century Nationalism** (SB) Answer Discussion Question Page 211 (LP) Optional **Lesson 32 Exam** 1 or 2 Page 289–290 (LP)			

Chapter 33: Urbanization: Sociological Advances

Between 1880 and 1900, cities in the United States grew at a dramatic rate. Noise, slums, air pollution, and sanitation issues became commonplace. The infrastructure of the 19th century city could not sustain this rapid urban growth.

	Day	Assignment			
	Day 161	Read **Lesson 1 — Overview** (SB) Answer Discussion Question Page 213 (LP)			
	Day 162	Read **Lesson 2 — Skyscrapers** (SB) Answer Discussion Question Page 214 (LP)			
Week 6	Day 163	Read **Lesson 3 — Boss Tweed** (SB) Answer Discussion Question Page 215 (LP)			
	Day 164	Read **Lesson 4 — The Great Chicago Fire** (SB) Answer Discussion Question Page 216 (LP)			
	Day 165	Read **Lesson 5 — Evangelical Social Welfare in the City** (SB) Answer Discussion Question Page 217 (LP) Optional **Lesson 33 Exam** 1 or 2 Page 291–292 (LP)			

Chapter 34: 1900: A New Century
A Southern African American woman; a Pennsylvania coal miner; a New York collar starcher; and a Midwest college professor's wife. Glimpse these journals of four courageous Americans, and be inspired by their voices.

Date	Day	Assignment	Due Date	✓	Grade
Week 7	Day 166	Read **Lesson 1 — 1900: Daily Life** (SB) Answer Discussion Question Page 219 (LP)			
	Day 167	Read **Lesson 2 — An Autobiography: A Southern . . . Woman** (SB) Answer Discussion Question Page 220 (LP)			
	Day 168	Read **Lesson 3 — A Miner's Story, (1902)** (SB) Answer Discussion Question Page 221 (LP)			
	Day 169	Read **Lesson 4 — A Collar Starcher's Story (1905)** (SB) Answer Discussion Question Page 222 (LP)			
	Day 170	Read **Lesson 5 — College Professor's Wife, Homeschool Mom** (SB) Answer Discussion Question Page 223 (LP) Optional **Lesson 34 Exam** 1 or 2 Page 293–294 (LP)			
		Semester Grade			

Daily Worksheets

Discussion Questions:

Why were medieval Europeans ready to explore the world?

Discussion Questions:

The Greenland Vikings were fervent churchgoers and built a fairly tidy European community. In fact, a woolen hood excavated from a churchyard in Greenland dating to the late 14th century showed that the Norsemen were even concerned about fashion! On the edge of nowhere, so-called rough Viking Greenlanders were keeping up with European fashion in the midst of a cooling climate and decreasing trade contacts! Why?

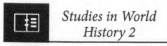
Discussion Questions:

While Prince Henry the Navigator never took a voyage and never received any accolades for his efforts, he was critical to the beginning of the Age of Exploration. Can you think of someone who has been critical to the success of a new endeavor but no one knew about his contribution?

Discussion Questions:

Is it wrong for a nation, a church, and an explorer who did not know better, who only acted like normal 15th-century Christian people, to make great monetary profits from inflicting great injustice and pain on people groups (slaves and Native Americans)?

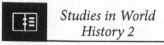
Discussion Questions:

What technological improvements helped Europeans explore their world?

Discussion Questions:

Why did the diversity among Native peoples prove to be their greatest weakness?

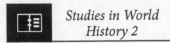

Discussion Questions:

There were great differences between Native American societies and European societies. But there were also great similarities. What were some of these similarities?

Discussion Questions:

How did kinship patterns benefit Native American people?

Discussion Questions:

In what ways did Native American government structures parallel European models?

Discussion Questions:

Give some contemporary examples of ethnocentricity.

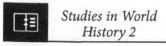
Discussion Questions:

Progress in all things is not inevitable. For instance, in mapmaking, Renaissance maps were inferior to earlier medieval maps. Why?

Discussion Questions:

Why was the myth of the Northwest Passage so enduring?

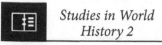
Discussion Questions:

Edward R. Shaw, the distinguished scholar and Dean of the School of Pedagogy, New York University, writes a fairly inaccurate summary of the Age of Exploration. The question arises, how could he say things like, "Four hundred years ago most of the people who lived in Europe thought that the earth was flat"? Other scholars at the time knew this to be inaccurate. Discuss some of the inaccuracies of this essay and why you think Dr. Shaw stated them.

Discussion Questions:

How does a historian know if a secondary source is valuable?

Discussion Questions:

When and why did the Age of Exploration end?

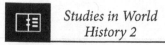
Discussion Questions:

What were some Native American stereotypes accepted by many Europeans?

Discussion Questions:

Why was French accommodation so successful?

Discussion Questions:

Why were the English unable to live peacefully with Native Americans?

Discussion Questions:

Why were European wars so devastating to North American Native Americans?

Discussion Questions:

What can we learn by studying the life of Lewis Wetzel?

Discussion Questions:

Why was the end of feudalism delayed so long in Russia?

Discussion Questions:

Nationalist, grassroots revolts are great, but what dangers do they engender (e.g., Napoleon)?

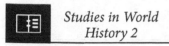
Discussion Questions:

In what way was European prosperity from 1500–1600 unlike any other previous economic boom?

Discussion Questions:

What causes premodern cities to grow, and why did their prosperity remain tied to agrarian industries?

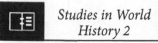
Discussion Questions:

Why are international wars rarely total wars?

Discussion Questions:

What problem does the author have with popular interpretations of the Renaissance?

Discussion Questions:

The Renaissance humanists defined the new movement initially as one that was different from the old-fashioned church. Thus they exhibited what is called a grievance mentality. What is the danger of defining a movement out of a grievance mentality?

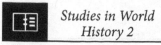
Discussion Questions:

Why did the Renaissance begin in Italy?

Discussion Questions:

What new contemporary invention has changed the course of history?

Discussion Questions:

The Northern Renaissance shows how social reforms can piggyback on cultural reform or aesthetic revivals. In other words the Renaissance, in the northern countries, tied itself with social reformers. Why does this naturally happen?

Discussion Questions:

How did the concept of art change during the Renaissance?

Discussion Questions:

What made Greek art different from other art in the ancient world?

Discussion Questions:

Who is your favorite artist of these three and why?

Discussion Questions:

Why was baroque so different from other Renaissance paintings?

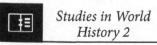

Discussion Questions:

According to Myers, what three changes did the Renaissance bring to Western society?

Discussion Questions:

What caused the Protestant Reformation?

Discussion Questions:

What were some of the theological issues that Martin Luther emphasized?

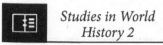
Discussion Questions:

The Thirty Years' War was the first war caused by religious conflict. It was not the last one. What are two or three contemporary examples of religious conflict?

Discussion Questions:

How did the Roman Catholic Church react to the Protestant Reformation?

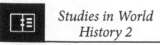
Discussion Questions:

Protestants argued that Scripture alone must be the thing to which other Scripture is compared. Roman Catholicism argued that Scripture, while it was inspired by the Holy Spirit, should be interpreted in light of earlier tradition. Summarize De Sales' argument against the Protestant understanding of the authority of Scripture. Which is more persuasive?

Discussion Questions:

To Woodrow Wilson, what are the main characteristics of government?

Discussion Questions:

Why were constitutional governments emerging?

Discussion Questions:

What allure did absolutism bring to most Europeans?

Discussion Questions:

Why is Hobbian philosophy so anti-Christian?

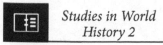

Discussion Questions:

What are some societal problems that could rise with moral absolutism?

Discussion Questions:

Religion and science had conflicts from 1450 to 1600. But, by and large, these two were able to cooperatively coexist. Why?

Discussion Questions:

What is the difference between deductive and inductive reasoning?

Discussion Questions:

What would be a satisfactory explanation of Joshua 10, where the sun stood still, that does not violate the truth of Scripture?

Discussion Questions:

Why do technological advances inevitably show up in weapon technology?

Discussion Questions:

When should technology be rejected?

Discussion Questions:

Why was there no antislavery movement in European history?

Discussion Questions:

What series of circumstances conspired to make Africa the idea genesis of New World slavery?

Discussion Questions:

How did Islam enhance the slave trade?

Discussion Questions:

Why was slavery such a lucrative business for all?

Discussion Questions:

Summarize the ordeal that slaves faced as they waited on the shores of West Africa to be deported to the New World.

Discussion Questions:

Why was chattel slavery so prevalent in the Americas?

Discussion Questions:

What four new, ominous developments occurred in New World slavery?

Discussion Questions:

In what ways did the slaves maintain their cultural identity as a way to sustain their sense of human dignity?

Discussion Questions:

Although slaves often outnumbered their owners, there were very few slave uprisings. Why?

Discussion Questions:

Compare slavery in Latin America with slavery in the United States.

Discussion Questions:

Who was Rienzi and why did he have such a great impact on history?

Discussion Questions:

Why, according to British historian Thomas Carlyle, did the Puritan Civil War/Revolution fail?

Discussion Questions:

Who were the Jacobites?

Discussion Questions:

How was the American Revolution far more than a war for independence?

Discussion Questions:

Why do reasonable, even necessary, revolts often turn into evil bloodbaths?

Discussion Questions:

The Herrnhut community often prayed Scripture. Offer a few suggestions.

Discussion Questions:

Why were the Anabaptists such a threat to other Christians?

Discussion Questions:

Why are the Puritans such popular targets of abuse? Why does America seem to need these targets?

Discussion Questions:

Compare these two interpretations of the First Great Awakening. Where do they agree? Where do they disagree?

Discussion Questions:

In general, what effect did the First Great Awakening have on the young American colonies?

Discussion Questions:

Despite the fact that Christian believers had no extant copies of the Old and New Testaments, and despite the fact that the Bible was written in languages not commonly used today, Christian believers are still confident that the Bible is accurate in historicity and in theology. Why?

Discussion Questions:

What is the canon and how did it miraculously emerge?

Discussion Questions:

Why did the Roman Catholic Church resist translation of the Bible from Latin to common languages (e.g., English)?

Discussion Questions:

Why is it ironic that the King James Bible is the most preferred Bible in the Protestant United States?

Discussion Questions:

Why does the author reject "lukewarm neutrality" on the issue of religion in history?

Discussion Questions:

What makes the Puritan experiment so unique in premodern history?

Discussion Questions:

How was the New England Confederation a prototype for later colonial unions?

Discussion Questions:

In 1620–1621, it was arguably Massasoit, chief of the Wampanoags, who saved the lives of the scarecrow Pilgrim survivors of the first winter at Plymouth. Yet, scarcely a generation later, Massasoit's son Philip suffered a terrible defeat. Philip was slain, his body drawn and quartered, and his head paraded in triumph in Plymouth. Philip's son, Massasoit's grandson, was sold into slavery in Bermuda. The generosity of Massasoit in 1620 indirectly resulted in the enslavement of his grandson 56 years later. Why?

Discussion Questions:

Why did religion diminish in importance in the Puritan colony, founded by Winthrop and his friends as a "city on a hill" to proclaim the goodness and love of the Lord Jesus Christ?

Discussion Questions:

With what part, if any, of the above essay will you disagree and why?

Discussion Questions:

How reliable do you think Moses' account of this military incident is? Give reasons for your response.

Discussion Questions:

What crisis did Jonathan Edwards find in his new church?

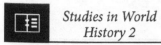

Discussion Questions:

Describe the indentured servitude that these German immigrants endured and explain why they would persevere through such hardship to come to the New World.

Discussion Questions:

Horsmanden ends the trial with the following statements that he gave to two convicted slaves:

> You both now stand convicted of one of the most horrid and detestable pieces of villainy, that ever satan instilled into the heart of human creatures to put in practice; ye, and the rest of your colour, though you are called slaves in this country; yet are you all far from the condition of other slaves in other countries; nay, your lot is superior to that of thousands of white people. You are furnished with all the necessaries of life, meat, drink, and clothing, without care, in a much better manner than you could provide for yourselves, were you at liberty; as the miserable condition of many free people here of your complexion might abundantly convince you. What then could prompt you to undertake so vile, so wicked, so monstrous, so execrable and hellish a scheme, as to murder and destroy your own masters and benefactors? nay, to destroy root and branch, all the white people of this place, and to lay the whole town in ashes. . . . I know not which is more astonishing, the extreme folly, or wickedness, of so base and shocking a conspiracy. . . . What could it be expected to end in, in the account of any rational and considerate person among you, but your own destruction.[1]

Why would these slaves commit these crimes?

---

1   findarticles.com/p/articles/mi_m0SAF/is_1_29/ai_n9772269; www.digitalhistory.uh.edu/

Discussion Questions:

What can you conclude about the average life of an 18th-century woman?

Discussion Questions:

In the middle of his career, Adams had a great falling out with his old friend, Thomas Jefferson. In 1796, Adams was elected president after serving two terms as vice president to Washington. His vice president was his friend Thomas Jefferson. By this point, though, the government was divided between the Federalists, the party of Adams, and the Republicans, led by Jefferson. The break between the two widened as Adams sought to keep America from becoming involved in a war with France. Adams' attempt to work out an agreement failed when Jefferson refused to go along with him. "The fact is," says one historian, "Jefferson wanted to have some sort of peace negotiation with France. But Jefferson wanted the Federalists to fail, and for the Federalists to fail, Adams had to fail." When Jefferson beat Adams in the election of 1800 it appeared that the rift was permanent. Jefferson spread spurious lies about Adams' character. Over the years, however, Adams' bitterness dissipated, and in 1812, he wrote a letter to Jefferson. "You and I ought not die before we have explained ourselves to each other," he wrote. Jefferson immediately wrote back. They began writing to each other — one hundred and fifty letters in all — and it became one of the greatest stories of reconciliation in American history. In October 1818, Abigail Adams was stricken with typhoid fever and died, just short of her 74th birthday. "God bless you and support you under your heavy affliction," Jefferson wrote. "While you live, I seem to have a bank at Monticello on which I can draw for a letter of friendship when I please," replied Adams. Both Adams and Jefferson would live nearly another eight years. They died on the same day, the 50th anniversary of the Declaration of Independence, July 4, 1826. Jefferson went first, hanging on as long as possible. Later that day in Massachusetts, Adams died, his last words being, "Thomas Jefferson still survives."

What causes a great man to forgive the greatest of injustices?

Discussion Questions:

Why does a nation forget its heroes and heroines, and how can they be reclaimed?

Discussion Questions:

Historian Walter Isaacson writes, "The most interesting thing that Franklin invented, and continually reinvented, was himself. America's first great publicist, he was consciously trying to create a new American archetype. In the process, he carefully crafted his own persona, portrayed it in public, and polished it for posterity. His guiding principle was a 'dislike of everything that tended to debase the spirit of the common people.' Few of his fellow founders felt this comfort with democracy so fully, and none so intuitively." Why was Franklin so able to champion the common man?

Discussion Questions:

How did Alexander Hamilton become so successful so quickly?

Discussion Questions:

Was Gouverneur Morris the ablest man at the convention? Why or why not?

Discussion Questions:

Why might superstitions have arisen around childbirth?

Discussion Questions:

Describe courtship in colonial America.

Discussion Questions:

Why were Puritan cemeteries regarded as "dormitories?"

Discussion Questions:

When does art cease to be art and become vulgar and irresponsible?

Discussion Questions:

How were 18th-century slave families different from other families?

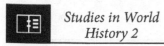

Discussion Questions:

The Battle of Narva was a tactical victory for the Swedes, but a strategic loss of far greater consequences would later ensue. Compare this to the American Revolution where the British won almost every battle but lost the war.

Discussion Questions:

Why was the Battle of Blenheim so important?

Discussion Questions:

Why was the Battle of Quebec a crucial 18th-century battle?

Discussion Questions:

Why was the 18th-century Battle of Lexington and Concord so important?

Discussion Questions:

What was the result of the Battle of Hohenlinden?

Discussion Questions:

What was the result of the Battle of Hohenlinden?

Discussion Questions:

This is one of the most disturbing essays that this author has read. Yet, it is probably true. What happens when mankind practices "God playing" or sees himself as more important than God?

Discussion Questions:

In your opinion (i.e., the answer is not in the above text), why do you think so much scientific progress was made in this century?

Discussion Questions:

How did Enlightenment thinkers handle Christianity?

Discussion Questions:

Joseph Priestley was a typical 19th-century scientist who maintained his faith while pursuing science. However, Priestley ultimately abandoned this orthodox faith in favor of heretical Unitarianism. How did this happen?

Discussion Questions:

How did Herschel discover the planet Uranus?

Discussion Questions:

How did Herschel discover the planet Uranus?

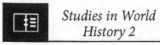
Discussion Questions:

While the readers are sympathetic with this heart-wrenching passage, they are forced to ask if this passage is accurate. Is it too prejudicial to be accurate? Do you believe this ex-slave could discuss his situation with anything that approaches objectivity?

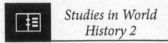

Discussion Questions:

List several reasons why Marquis de la Galissonière believes that the French are superior to the English in North America.

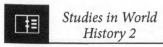
Discussion Questions:

What advice does Wadsworth offer to husbands and wives?

Discussion Questions:

Compare your own school curricula choices with the curricula at Boston Latin.

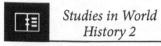
Discussion Questions:

This poem was popular among German armies in the 18th, 19th, and 20th centuries. What are militaristic images that Schneckenburger presents?

Discussion Questions:

Discuss the crisis facing America in the 1780s.

Discussion Questions:

Summarize the major components of the Articles of Confederation.

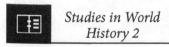
Discussion Questions:

By the mid 1780s, many of the country's most influential leaders became convinced that state legislatures had become the greatest source of tyranny in America. Why?

Discussion Questions:

By 1687, why did most of the American leadership feel that something must be done?

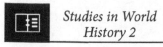
Discussion Questions:

In the midst of crises, other problems still exist. The Articles of Confederation precipitated a political crisis, but there were social problems that remained untouched. Summarize what Abigail Adams, John Adams, and Quock Case wrote. What important social issues remained to be solved?

Discussion Questions:

What bothersome paradox was emerging in pre-Revolutionary American society?

Discussion Questions:

Why was there so little opposition to slavery?

Discussion Questions:

Why did colonial conflicts emerge in the years before the American Revolution?

Discussion Questions:

Do you agree with Eric Williams' assessment of slavery?

Discussion Questions:

How was the 1790 law changed in 1795?

Discussion Questions:

Why does Guyon argue that prayer is for everyone?

Discussion Questions:

Why would Wheatley say this? "'Twas mercy brought me from my Pagan land."

Discussion Questions:

Describe several metaphors Rossetti uses to describe her relationship with God.

Discussion Questions:

What does Smith learn from her agnostic friend?

Discussion Questions:

Why is the author so hopeful?

Name	Date	Chapter 25 Lesson 5

Discussion Questions:

Why is the author so hopeful?

Discussion Questions:

In his contemporary (for his age) rendition of the New Testament, Thomas Jefferson removed the Resurrection. Why?

Discussion Questions:

What does Hume say about religion?

Discussion Questions:

Discuss Paine's views on religion.

Discussion Questions:

English poet Joseph Addison celebrates natural scenes as a foil to deism and romanticism emerging in late 18th-century Europe. Can you note at least three examples of this?

Discussion Questions:

Write a letter to someone who has encouraged you in your Christian walk.

Discussion Questions:

The 19th century was full of contradictions. How?

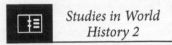
Discussion Questions:

Why was Russia so resistant to democratic reforms spreading across Europe?

Discussion Questions:

What caused the Ottoman Empire to fall?

Discussion Questions:

What was the fundamental reason that the Austro-Hungarian Empire declined so precipitously during the 19th century?

Discussion Questions:

Name another country, another age, whose identity was tied completely to the image and soul of one person, like England was bound to its Queen Victoria.

Discussion Questions:

Why did the unification of Germany cause such consternation in the foreign policy ministries of Europe?

Discussion Questions:

Why did Italian unity come so late?

Discussion Questions:

What were the four goals of the Congress of Vienna and to what degree were these goals met?

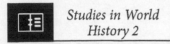
Discussion Questions:

Why was it ironic that an ultra conservative was elected in France in the wake of the liberal revolution of 1848? How did this happen?

Discussion Questions:

Why was Alfred Dreyfus charged for treason?

Discussion Questions:

Discuss the state of the family in 19th-century America.

Discussion Questions:

What replaces the dependency between generations that existed in the 18th century?

Discussion Questions:

What three types of families does Greven argue were present in 19th-century America?

Discussion Questions:

Why was transcendentalism such a threat to Christianity?

Discussion Questions:

Paraphrase this scene of the last moments of a slave's life.

Discussion Questions:

What is the main reason President Polk declared war against Mexico?

Discussion Questions:

This speech expresses strong opinions about God's providence. What does Lincoln say?

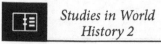

Discussion Questions:

What argument does Bismarck offer to the Prussian Landtag to convince them to fund an expanding army?

Discussion Questions:

Many consider this short farewell speech to be the best of its genre. Why?

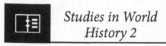

Discussion Questions:

Why does Chief Joseph decide to give up, finally, in his fight against the United States?

Discussion Questions:

In what ways does the life of Manjiro shadow the Japanese-American relations?

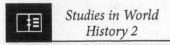

Discussion Questions:

Why did Japanese populate the Hawaiian Islands?

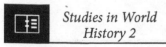
Discussion Questions:

What reason does Chew offer that Chinese immigrants often started laundry businesses?

Discussion Questions:

Why were Chinese workers brought into America to build the Transcontinental Railroad?

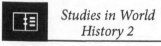
Discussion Questions:

Describe the prejudice, violence, and discriminatory practices faced by 1860 Chinese immigrants in California.

Discussion Questions:

Evaluate (i.e., is it a good thing and why) nationalism as a historical phenomenon.

Discussion Questions:

Discuss the distinctive of romanticism.

Discussion Questions:

How was the development of the Gothic romance tied to nationalism?

Discussion Questions:

Nationalism showed a nasty side in the Franco-Prussian War. How would you describe it?

Discussion Questions:

Compare and contrast these examples of nationalism.

Discussion Questions:

Why did cities grow so rapidly at the end of the 19th century?

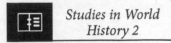

Discussion Questions:

Why was a skyscraper such an appealing technology?

Discussion Questions:

Why did men like Tweed gain such power in cities?

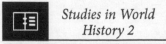
Discussion Questions:

Discuss the cause and impact of the Chicago fire.

Discussion Questions:

Describe the late 19th-century evangelical movement and the impact it had on cities.

Discussion Questions:

When I was a little boy, my dad regularly took our family, three boys and a wife, forty-five minutes to eat at a new restaurant called "McDonalds" north of Pine Bluff, Arkansas. What a treat! The hamburgers were a little pricey — $.25 — and you could only have catsup on them — every southerner knows that mayonnaise and lots of it is the best thing to put on all sandwiches — but it was fun driving our 1957 Chevrolet Belair up Highway 65 with the windows down (because we had no air conditioning) trying to survive my parents' nasty smoking habits and my older brother's nasty stomach problems.

Once, as we sojourned up 65, we spied a new store that had just opened. In blue and white letters was "Walmart." It was just across the street from the Admiral Benbow Hotel, Pine Bluff, Arkansas. We were skeptical, but we thought we would give it a try. We were looking to buy some new duck decoys since our other ones were dry rotted. We went into the store, and I will never forget the experience. It was like I had lived all my life in the third world of West Department Store or the dime store or other little, uncluttered stores where one had virtually no selection at all. I have to tell you, it was completely disorienting suddenly to have forty-five choices of everything one might want. There were, for instance, at least, four different choices of Lucky 13 lures in the sporting goods' section. The ebullience of this place was overwhelming. My dad, who was used to the brotherly care of Mr. Huddleston and Mr. Stuart who ran the local Sportsman's Center, and always preferred a friendly handshake and smile to any old bargain, quickly looked for a salesman to help us. What he found was a lady. Yes, a lady was employed to help us in the sportsman section of a 1960ish Walmart. Poor Dad first asked to speak to the sales clerk's husband, but, discovering that the poor thing was a spinster — and no wonder, she was very rude to my dad. What poor soul would want to marry that lady? In great frustration, he gave up and purposed to wait and see if Mr. Huddleston and Mr. Stuart might have what he wanted. As we left the store, I distinctly remembering my dad shaking his head, feeling genuine pity for the Walmart folks, who Dad knew were decent folks "Jimmy, take note. This store will never make it. Walmart will be out of business in a year." Of course, he was wrong. What 1900 food choices and other cultural phenomenon have survived, and which ones have disappeared?

Discussion Questions:

What sort of indignities did African-Americans have to endure?

Discussion Questions:

Why did this miner strike?

Discussion Questions:

How is the woman conflicted?

Discussion Questions:

Why does this courageous mom homeschool?

Chapter Exam Section

Fill in the blanks with words from the following list:

Astrolabe

Caravel

L'Anse aux Meadows

Lead Line

Mariner's Compass

1. _____ The Newfoundland Viking settlement.

2. _____ Fast, technological advanced ships that expanded exploration overseas.

3. _____ A more advanced compass used to navigate ships.

4. _____ Used to measure the depth of water.

5. _____ A navigation tool to calculate longitude and latitude of ships.

Short Answer Essay:

Google.com has invented technology that will allow iPhones to take pictures of people and from those pictures give the addresses and phone numbers of the people in the picture. Is this right? Are there some technologies that we should choose not to use?

Fill in the blanks with words from the following list:

Eastern Woodlands

Ethnocentrism

Homogeneous population

Warrior chiefs

The Iroquois League

1. _____ A group of people with similar traits.

2. _____ A forested area stretching from the Atlantic coast west to the Great Lakes and southward from Maine to North Carolina.

3. _____ Leaders chosen for their bravery, acumen, and style.

4. _____ Combined a central authority with tribal autonomy and provided a model for the federal system of government later adopted by the United States.

5. _____ Making value judgments about another culture from the perspective of one's own culture.

Short Answer Essay:

Far from being "primitive" forms of religion, Indian religions possessed great subtlety and sophistication, manifest in a rich ceremonial life, an intricate mythology, and profound speculations about the creation of the world, the origins of life, and the nature of the afterlife. Design an evangelism strategy to convert the Native Americans.

Fill in the blanks with words from the following list:

Age of Exploration
Cartography
Northwest Passage
Primary source
Secondary source

1. _____ The science of mapmaking.

2. _____ An alleged shortcut from Europe to the Orient by going west.

3. _____ An era of vigorous exploration of the New World.

4. _____ A document that is firsthand information, found to be more reliable.

5. _____ A document that is based on secondhand information and not considered as reliable.

Short Answer Essay:

Why would this short history of Sir Francis Drake by Professor Shaw, *Discoverers and Explorers* (1900), be of dubious value?

Fill in the blanks with words from the following list:

Accommodation

Jamestown

Nation building

Stereotype

William Penn

1. _____ Oversimplified types.

2. _____ To participate or to cooperate with competing forces.

3. _____ Act of building a nation usually in the spirit and image of the creating institution.

4. _____ The first permanent English settlement.

5. _____ Founder of the Quakers.

Short Answer Essay:

In 1783, the United States was a new nation of about three million people living, for the most part, along the Atlantic seaboard. Native Americans, perhaps numbering around 600,000, controlled most lands west of the Appalachian Mountains. By 1890, a bit more than a century later, the United States stretched from coast to coast and was home to some 66 million people. Only 250,000 Indians remained, most of them living on reservations holding just a fraction of the land they once controlled. What caused this to occur and what patterns are established in 18th-century America?

Fill in the blanks with words from the following list:

Capital accumulation

Duman

Nationalist revolts

Technological innovation

Total war

1. _____ Russian legislative branch.

2. _____ Revolutions stimulated by nationalist agendas.

3. _____ Technological, scientific advances related to new products.

4. _____ The collection of wealth for investment.

5. _____ A war that affects soldiers and civilians.

Short Answer Essay:

Development in early, or premodern, Europe was profound. Europe's world prestige shifted significantly as the New World was explored and exploited. A plethora of new industries appeared that profoundly affected the European economy. Feudalism shifted to paid labor. The scientific revolution affected all aspects of life, including farming, and its success assured the success of premodern European economies. Strong, national economies were protected by strong monarchies and strong armies. All this largesse and growth was dependent, however, on the lowly farmer. Explain.

Fill in the blanks with words from the following list:

Desiderius Erasmus

Grievance mentality

Humanists

Johannes Gutenberg

Renaissance

1. _____ Scholars who focused on classic works and human achievement.

2. _____ A mindset that reacts against a certain notion or philosophy.

3. _____ Used movable type to print papal documents and the first printed version of the Bible.

4. _____ Literally means "rebirth."

5. _____ A Dutch humanist.

Short Answer Essay:

Comment on the following quote from an 1888 book on the Renaissance:

The great achievements of the Renaissance were the discovery of the world and the discovery of man. Under these two formula may be classified all the phenomena which properly belong to this period. The discovery of the world divides itself into two branches — the exploration of the globe, and that systematic exploration of the universe, which is in fact what we call Science. Columbus made known America in 1492; the Portuguese rounded the Cape in 1497; Copernicus explained the solar system in 1507. It is not necessary to add anything to this plain statement; for, in contact with facts of such momentous import, to avoid what seems like commonplace reflection would be difficult. Yet it is only when we contrast the ten centuries which preceded these dates with the four centuries which have ensued, that we can estimate the magnitude of that Renaissance movement by means of which a new hemisphere has been added to civilization. In like manner, it is worthwhile to pause a moment and consider what is implied in the substitution of the Copernican for the Ptolemaic system. The world, regarded in old times as the center of all things, the apple of God's eye, for the sake of which were created sun and moon and stars, suddenly was found to be one of the many balls that roll round a giant sphere of light and heat, which is itself but one among innumerable suns attended each by a cortège of planets, and scattered, how we know not, through infinity. What has become of that brazen seat of the old gods, that Paradise to which an ascending Deity might be caught up through clouds, and hidden for a moment from the eyes of his disciples. The demonstration of the simplest truths of astronomy destroyed at a blow the legends that were most significant to the early Christians by annihilating their symbolism. Well might the Church persecute Galileo for his proof of the world's mobility. Instinctively she perceived that in this one proposition was involved the principle of hostility to her most cherished conceptions, to the very core of her mythology. Science was born, and the warfare between scientific positivism and religious metaphysic was declared. (John Symonds, Renaissance in Italy, NY: Holt, Co., 1888, p. 16)

Fill in the blanks with words from the following list:

Aesthetic

Baroque

Beaux-Art

Chiaroscuro

Parthenon

1. _____ Art whose sole purpose is to bring beauty vs. art to glorify God.

2. _____ Art appreciation.

3. _____ Greek Athenian temple.

4. _____ A "modern" artistic style that emphasized light and shadow.

5. _____ Gold highlighting in Renaissance painting.

Short Answer Essay:

The classical concept of beaux-arts, a term that was coined in France during the 18th century, was reclaimed in the Renaissance. The arts of the beautiful were separated from the arts of the useful because of the belief that the fine arts had a special quality: they served to give pleasure to an audience. The type of pleasure was called aesthetic, and it referred to the satisfaction given to the individual or group solely from perceiving — seeing or hearing — a work of art. Is the notion that a piece of art should be beautiful a good or bad concept?

Fill in the blanks with words from the following list:

Anabaptists

John Calvin

John Knox

Martin Luther

Pope Leo X

1. _____ Started the Protestant Reformation.
2. _____ The pope who confronted Luther.
3. _____ Swiss reformer who championed the Reformed position.
4. _____ A Scottish reformer.
5. _____ Early dissenters who preferred believer baptism and pacifism.

Short Answer Essay:

The Protestant reformers found a cause worth dying for. What contemporary Christian cause is worth dying for and why?

Fill in the blanks with words from the following list:

Absolutism

Authority

Constitutional governments

Moral absolutism

Peace of Westphalia

1. _____ Government by consent of the governed through written documents.

2. _____ The treaty that ended the Thirty Years' War.

3. _____ Society controlled completely by one person or small group.

4. _____ The essential characteristic of all government, whatever its form.

5. _____ Government that makes all the choices for everyone.

Short Answer Essay:

What is the biblical view of government?

Fill in the blanks with words from the following list:

Copernicus

Epistemology

Imperialism

The deductive approach

The inductive approach

1. _____ The study of knowledge.

2. _____ Starts with commonsense observations and moves toward complex conclusions.

3. _____ Starts with objective facts.

4. _____ A scientist who argued that the sun, not the earth, was the center of the universe.

5. _____ The policy of extending the rule or influence of a country over other countries or colonies.

Short Answer Essay:

Concerning Galileo, why was it so difficult for the Church to accept the obvious truth that the Earth rotated around the sun?

Fill in the blanks with words from the following list:

Atlantic slave trade

Islamic traders

Manumission

Slave trades

Sub-Saharan Africa

1. _____ To free from slavery.

2. _____ Below the Sahara Desert.

3. _____ Islamic commercial traders, mostly in slaves.

4. _____ A slave business administered by Europeans between the West Indies and Africa.

5. _____ Contributed to the development of powerful African states.

Short Answer Essay:

How can civilized, Christian nations sanction, even encourage chattel slavery? Of course slavery is justified by Scripture (at least in the eyes of slavery apologists), but still, how can Christians examine and support such heinous crimes?

Fill in the blanks with words from the following list:

Chattel slavery

Indentured servants

Maroon colonies

Plantations

Race mixing

1. _____ Agricultural businesses that raised valuable crops.

2. _____ Servants who were obligated to work for a few years but then were freed.

3. _____ Colonies full of racially mixed people.

4. _____ Marriage across racial lines.

5. _____ Slaves are considered as "chattel" or personal property.

Short Answer Essay:

If you were part of a persecuted Christian minority, perhaps even a slave society, what sort of rituals and cultural practices would you maintain that would not antagonize your owners?

Fill in the blanks with words from the following list:

Cola di Rienzi

House of Hanover

Natural rights

Papacy

Popular sovereignty

1. _____ The pope and his office.

2. _____ An Italian nobleman who really wanted the papacy returned to Rome.

3. _____ Replaced the Stuarts in the monarchy of England.

4. _____ Government instituted for the right of people, not the government.

5. _____ Rights given by God, not by man.

Short Answer Essay:

Were the great revolutions of the 18th century successful?

Fill in the blanks with words from the following list:

Anabaptists

Count Nikolaus Ludwig von Zinzendorf

Herrnhut

Manifest Destiny

Moravian Church

1. _____ A Moravian nobleman who started the Herrnhut communities.

2. _____ A pietistic, 1700 church.

3. _____ Moravian communities famous for missionary work and a 100-year prayer meeting.

4. _____ Radicals who embraced pacifism and believer baptism.

5. _____ The view that Americans were destined to rule the North American continent.

Short Answer Essay:

Read the following concerning the First Great Awakening and answer the accompanying question.

Benjamin Franklin's Autobiography[1]

In 1739 arrived among us from Ireland the Reverend Mr. Whitefield, who had made himself remarkable there as an itinerant preacher. He was at first permitted to preach in some of our churches; but the clergy, taking a dislike to him, soon refus'd him their pulpits, and he was oblig'd to preach in the fields. The multitudes of all sects and denominations that attended his sermons were enormous, and it was matter of speculation to me, who was one of the number, to observe the extraordinary influence of his oratory on his hearers, and how much they admir'd and respected him, notwithstanding his common abuse of them, by assuring them that they were naturally half beasts and half devils. It was wonderful to see the change soon made in the manners of our inhabitants. From being thoughtless or indifferent about religion, it seem'd as if all the world were growing religious, so that one could not walk thro' the town in an evening without hearing psalms sung in different families of every street. . . .

Mr. Whitefield, in leaving us, went preaching all the way thro' the colonies to Georgia. The settlement of that province had lately been begun, but, instead of being made with hardy, industrious husbandmen, accustomed to labor, the only people fit for such an enterprise, it was with families of broken shop-keepers and other insolvent debtors, many of indolent and idle habits, taken out of the jails, who, being set down in the woods, unqualified for clearing land, and unable to endure the hardships of a new settlement, perished in numbers, leaving many helpless children unprovided for. The sight of their miserable situation inspir'd the benevolent heart of Mr. Whitefield with the idea of building an Orphan House there, in which they might be supported and educated. Returning northward, he preach'd up this charity, and made large collections, for his eloquence had a wonderful power over the hearts and purses of his hearers, of which I myself was an instance.

I did not disapprove of the design, but, as Georgia was then destitute of materials and workmen, and it was proposed to send them from Philadelphia at a great expense, I thought it would have been better to have built the house here, and brought the children to it. This I advis'd; but he was resolute in his first project, rejected my counsel, and I therefore refus'd to contribute. I happened soon after to attend one of his sermons, in the course of which I perceived he intended to finish with a collection, and I silently resolved he should get nothing from me, I had in my pocket a handful of copper money, three or four silver dollars, and five pistoles in gold. As he proceeded I began to soften, and concluded to give the coppers. Another stroke of his oratory made me asham'd of that, and determin'd me to give the silver; and he finish'd so admirably, that I empty'd my pocket wholly into the collector's dish, gold and all.

Ben Franklin was a good friend of George Whitefield, though he did not agree with his religious beliefs. Many historians question if Benjamin Franklin was even a born-again Christian, yet, he deeply respected and admired the evangelist George Whitfield. Why?

---

1   The Autobiography of Benjamin Franklin, 1793.

Fill in the blanks with words from the following list:

Athanasius

Geneva Bible

King James Bible

Latin Vulgate Bible

Septuagint

1. _____ The Old Testament in Greek.

2. _____ An early Roman Catholic Bible.

3. _____ An early Protestant translation.

4. _____ The official British government translation in the early 17th century.

5. _____ Christian theologian, bishop of Alexandria, Church Father, and noted Egyptian leader.

Short Answer Essay:

James, reluctantly, with very little enthusiasm, desired to secure reconciliation between the throne and the Anglican church on the one hand, and the Puritans on the other. Therefore as he traveled from Scotland to London to assume the throne, he called the Hampton Court Conference in January of 1604 "for the hearing, and for the determining, things pretended to be amiss in the church" inviting Anglican bishops, along with four Puritan leaders, to consider the complaints of the Puritans. None of the Puritan demands were met but one. The Puritan president of Corpus Christi College, John Reynolds, "moved his Majesty, that there might be a new translation of the Bible, because those which were allowed in the reigns of Henry the eighth, and Edward the sixth, were corrupt and not answerable to the truth of the Original." King James did that and changed the course of history. Offer other examples or reluctant leaders who nonetheless changed the course of history.

Fill in the blanks with words from the following list:

Covenant

Hartford Convention

Massachusetts Declaration of Rights of 1661

Sir Edmund Andros

Wampanoags

1. _____ A contract between two consenting parties.

2. _____ A 19th-century declaration of independence, of sorts, by New England.

3. _____ Native people in New England.

4. _____ A statement of English rights.

5. _____ Controversial English governor in New England.

Short Answer Essay:

One historian writes, "Today the term Puritan is often applied to various manifestations of American life. A strict parent is 'puritanical.' Sometimes the allusion is merely metaphoric, suggesting similarities between some aspect of current behavior and the ways of the New England colonists. But those who see 'Puritan' traits in the lineaments of later America often go further to maintain that an actual connection exists between later American development and its Puritan heritage. In a recent study of the genesis of the American mind, Max Savelle finds Puritanism '. . . firmly rooted in the American experience and in the emerging American mind of the eighteenth century, and from New England as a center it has radiated its influence in American civilization, for good or ill, from that day to this; and the end is not yet.' Ralph Barton Perry concludes that 'The Puritans imprinted on English and American institutions a quality of manly courage, self-reliance, and sobriety. We are still drawing upon the reserves of spiritual vigor which they accumulated.' In fact, the postulate that Puritanism has been one of the principal influences in the development of American civilization is an assumption rarely questioned by writers of our history." Discuss some of the political institutions, morals, and social structures that exist today that can be traced to Bay Colony and Puritanism.

Fill in the blanks with words from the following list:

Gottlieb Mittelberger

History

Mary Cooper

Redemptioners

Seven Years' War

1. _____ The French and Indian War between France and England (primarily).

2. _____ A kind of indentured servant.

3. _____ A collection of individual narratives.

4. _____ Began her diary at age 54 while tending the family farmstead with her husband.

5. _____ A schoolteacher who left his wife and children to travel to America.

Short Answer Essay:

Americans are prone to romanticizing the past and confusing historical fantasy and reality. This is especially true when Americans ponder the 17th century, the century that spawned George Washington and Benjamin Franklin. But they were the minority. This week we read entries from ordinary Americans, whose hopes and dreams built a nation and a world. What makes these primary sources so important?

Fill in the blanks with words from the following list:

Boston Massacre

Constitutional Convention

Continental Congress in 1782

Declaration of Independence

Sons of Liberty

1. _____ A 1770 incident where British soldiers fired on American citizens.

2. _____ A secret organization of American patriots.

3. _____ A declaration of American rights written in 1776.

4. _____ A meeting to write a new constitution.

5. _____ The ruling national legislature at the end of the American Revolution.

Short Answer Essay:

These Founding Fathers were not all saints. For example, most historians, even the most ardent patriot, admit that Franklin's moral life was appalling. He was a injudicious drinker and a notorious womanizer. Yet, he is one of America's premier patriots. How does one reconcile Franklin's capable leadership and his reprehensible moral behavior?

Fill in the blanks with words from the following list:

Courtship

East

Mayflower

Midwives

Vacation

1. _____ The ship that brought the Pilgrims to Plymouth.

2. _____ Social relation to prepare for marriage.

3. _____ An interlude, rest away from work.

4. _____ Older women who relied on practical experience in delivering children.

5. _____ Original headstones faced this direction awaiting the Day of Resurrection.

Short Answer Essay:

Men's and women's domestic roles are not ordained by human nature, biology, or men's and women's psychology. Rather, they are the product of particular historical circumstances, social processes, and ideologies, and vary widely by race, religion, and time period. Compare the 18th-century family with a contemporary family.

Fill in the blanks with words from the following list:

Battle of Blenheim

Battle of Hohenlinden

Battle of Lexington and Concord

Battle of Narva

Battle of Quebec

1. _____ That battle that showed Sweden was a major power.

2. _____ The battle that ended French domination of the continent until Napoleon.

3. _____ The battle that assured English domination of North America.

4. _____ The battle that precipitated the American Revolution.

5. _____ Napoleon's France was the premier power of Europe again.

Short Answer Essay:

The 18th century saw the end of chivalric knights and ushered in the 'Age of Rifles'. Discuss what new differences emerged.

Fill in the blanks with words from the following list:

Dissenters
Enlightenment
Jacques Turgot
Karl Linnaeus
Theory of Evolution

1. _____ A period of great progress in science and knowledge in general.
2. _____ A theory about the origin of species.
3. _____ Invented a classification for living things.
4. _____ French social thinker and economist.
5. _____ The Dissenters were a sort of Unitarian Universalist church.

Short Answer Essay:

No doubt, 18th-century scientists were men of hope. The age lent itself to hope. And of course, life spans increased. Real wealth increased. At the same time, enlightened thinkers ridiculed religion and extolled the virtues of humanitarianism. The point is this — 18th-century man was alienated from his God. He found himself disconnected from the warm, familiar idealism of evangelicalism, and therefore lost in the universe. He found himself, but lost his God and his way in the cosmos. An old professor of mine, Harvey Cox, once lamented, "Once mankind had imagination, dreams, and no technology. Now he has technology but no imagination or dreams." Is Professor Cox right? Give a contemporary example.

Fill in the blanks with words from the following list:

Boston Latin Grammar School

Jean le Rond d'Alembert

Marquis de la Galissonière

Max Schneckenburger

Olaudah Equiano

1. _____ A former slave who wrote narrative stories about his slave experience.

2. _____ French nobleman who wrote about New France.

3. _____ One of the first public schools.

4. _____ German poet.

5. _____ French philosopher.

Short Answer Essay:

Samuel Sewall (March 28, 1652 – January 1, 1730) was a Massachusetts judge, best known for his involvement in the Salem witch trials, for which he later apologized, and his essay "The Selling of Joseph (1700)," which criticized slavery.

> And all thing considered, it would conduce more to the Welfare of the Province, to have White Servants for a Term of Years, than to have Slaves for Life. Few can endure to hear of a Negro's being made free; and indeed they can seldom use their freedom well; yet their continual aspiring after their forbidden, renders them Unwilling Servants. And there is such a disparity in their Conditions, Color & Hair, that they can never embody with us, and grow up into orderly Families, to the Peopling of the Land: but still remain in our Body Politic as a kind of extravasat Blood. As many Negro men as there are among us, so many empty places there are in our Train Bands, and the places taken up of Men that might make Husbands for our Daughters. And the Sons and Daughters of New England would become more like Jacob, and Rachel, if this Slavery were thrust quite out of doors. . . It seems to be practically pleaded that they might be Lawless . . . It is likewise most lamentable to think, how in taking Negros out of Africa, and selling of them here, That which GOD has joined together men to boldly rend asunder; Men from their Country, Husbands from their Wives, Parents from their Children. How horrible is the Uncleanness, Mortality, if not Murder, that the Ships are guilty of that bring great Crowds of these miserable Men, and Women. Methinks, when we are bemoaning the barbarous Usage of our Friends and Kinsfolk in Africa: it might not be unseasonable to enquire whether we are not culpable in forcing the Africans to become Slaves amongst ourselves. And it may be a questions whether all the Benefit received by Negro Slaves, will balance the account of Cash laid out upon them; and for the Redemption of our own enslaved Friends out of Africa. Besides all the Persons and Estates that have perished there.

What are some of the arguments that Sewall offers against slavery?

Fill in the blanks with words from the following list:

Articles of Confederation

Democratic republic

Shays' Rebellion

State sovereignty

The Declaration of Independence

1. _____ American government until 1789.

2. _____ A rebellion caused by dysfunctional nature of the Articles of Confederation.

3. _____ Form of government elected by the people to represent them.

4. _____ States have governing authority over that of a central government.

5. _____ Document that established a foundation for U.S. governance.

Short Answer Essay:

By the end of the 1780s the nation was in turmoil. On hearing of Shays' rebellion, he exclaimed: "What, gracious God, is man that there should be such inconsistency and perfidiousness in his conduct! It is but the other day that we were shedding our blood to obtain the constitutions under which we now live — constitutions of our own choice and making — and now we are unsheathing our sword to overturn them." The same year he burst out in a lament over rumors of restoring royal government. "I am told that even respectable characters speak of a monarchical government without horror. From thinking proceeds speaking. Hence to acting is often but a single step. But how irresistible and tremendous! What a triumph for our enemies to verify their predictions! What a triumph for the advocates of despotism to find that we are incapable of governing ourselves!" The nation was ready for something different; the nation was ready for a constitutional convention. Offer other instances in history where something bad happens, but it leads to something good.

Fill in the blanks with words from the following list:

Eric Williams

John Woolman

Peter Zenger

Quaker opposition

Toussaint Louverture

1. _____ First major freedom of the press trial in America.

2. _____ Early American abolitionist.

3. _____ Leader of Haitian Revolution.

4. _____ These Christians founded the first American antislavery group.

5. _____ Wrote the book *Capitalism and Slavery*.

Short Answer Essay:

The generation that emerged 15 years before the American Revolution embraced noble causes, pursued idealistic goals. Today, many social historians argue that "idealism is dead." People, even young people, are full of cynicism and hopelessness. Why? And what could turn this around?

Fill in the blanks with words from the following list:

Christina Rossetti

Hanna Smith

Madame Guyon

Phillis Wheatley

Quietism

1. _____ A great woman of intercessory prayer.
2. _____ A slave poet of great ability.
3. _____ A British writer and saint.
4. _____ A great woman of holiness and faith.
5. _____ An assertive sort of passive resistance.

Short Answer Essay:

A historian has noted: "The way in which the Church began to lift woman up into privilege and hope was one of its most prompt and beautiful transformations from the blight of paganism. Too long in the darkness, she was now helped into the sunlight." Such a transformation impressed the unsaved world and brought many to a saving relationship with Jesus Christ. This winsome attitude progressed into the 20th century and did much to change the course of history. Clearly, in the matter of salvation, men and women both stand on equal footing before God. Paul says: "[T]here can be no male and female; for ye all are one in Christ Jesus" (Galatians 3:28). Yes, there are differences. What are these differences and how are they played out in history?

Fill in the blanks with words from the following list:

David Hume

John Wesley

The Jefferson Bible

Thomas Paine

William Wilberforce

1. _____ An interpretation of Scripture that removed references to the miracles and divinity of Christ.

2. _____ A philosopher who questioned the existence of miracles.

3. _____ An opportunistic atheist and capable writer.

4. _____ Father of the United Methodist Church.

5. _____ British statesman who ended slavery expansion in England.

Short Answer Essay:

18th-century writings concerning problems of religion are among the most important and influential contributions on this topic. In these writings Hume, Jefferson, and Paine advance a systematic, skeptical critique of the philosophical foundations of Christianity. They attempt to unmask and discredit the doctrines and dogmas of orthodox religious belief. What attacks do you hear today?

Fill in the blanks with words from the following list:

Colonization	Industrial Revolution
Crimean War of 1853–56	Laborer
Czar Alexander II	Middle class entrepreneur
Duma	Revolutions in 1848
Franz Joseph	Russo-Japanese War of 1904–05

1. _____ European nationalist revolutions in 1848.
2. _____ Movement that began in England but spread to the whole world.
3. _____ European policy of expansion.
4. _____ Important socio-economic class that grew powerful in the 18th century.
5. _____ A new class of people who were employed in factories.
6. _____ War between Russia and England and her western allies.
7. _____ 19th-century Russian Emperor.
8. _____ A complete victory of the Japanese over the Russians.
9. _____ Russian parliament.
10. _____ Habsburg dynasty monarch who ruled the Austro-Hungarian Empire for over 50 years.

Short Answer Essay:

19th-century Europe essentially engaged in an attempt to deal with the legacy of the French Revolution in 1789. The French opened a Pandora's Box that could not be closed. There were at least half a dozen great issues claiming attention and arousing passion. What were they?

Fill in the blanks with words from the following list:

Alfred Dreyfus

Archduke Maximilian

Congress Of Vienna

Giuseppe Garibaldi

Otto von Bismarck

1. _____ Great nationalist leader of Greater Germany.

2. _____ Italian patriot who unified Italy into a nation/state.

3. _____ Ended the Napoleonic wars.

4. _____ Austrian who ruled Mexico with French support.

5. _____ Jewish French officer unjustly charged for treason.

Short Answer Essay:

The 19th century begins with Napoleon Bonaparte rising to power in the aftermath of the French Revolution and established the First French Empire that, during the Napoleonic Wars, grew to encompass large parts of Europe before collapsing in 1815 with the Battle of Waterloo. A balance of power (of sorts) emerged that would remain until the Revolutions of 1848, during which liberal uprisings affected all of Europe except for Russia and Great Britain. These revolutions were eventually put down by conservative elements and few reforms resulted. Europe's population doubled during the 18th century, from roughly 100 million to almost 200 million, and doubled again during the 19th century. 70 million people immigrated to the United States. Compare the political climate in 8th-century Europe to 19th-century Europe.

Fill in the blanks with words from the following list:

Abolitionists

Corporal punishment

Ralph Waldo Emerson

Transcendentalism

Unitarian Church

1. _____ Antislavery activists.

2. _____ 19th century movement that celebrated the subjective and nature.

3. _____ Physical penalty or pain used to deter or discipline a child.

4. _____ Founded by the transcendentalists.

5. _____ A leading proponent of transcendentalism.

Short Answer Essay:

Some historians (e.g., Philip Greven) argue that only in the middle of the 19th century did ideas of affectionate marriages and loving, sentimental relations with children become dominant in American family life. These attitudes first took hold among the urban, educated wealthy and middle classes, and later spread to rural and poorer Americans. This change was due to the growth and increasing sophistication of the economy, which meant that economic issues became less pressing for families and production moved outside the home to specialized shops and factories. With more leisure time and greater physical comfort, people felt that happiness, rather than simple survival, was possible. Other historians (e.g., Perry Miller) argue that such views are spurious. They argue that to see 18th-century, mostly evangelical marriages to be "sterile" would be a misreading of evangelicalism. What do you think?

Fill in the blanks with words from the following list:

Abraham Lincoln

Chief Joseph

James K. Polk

Otto von Bismarck

Robert E. Lee

1. _____ President of the United States who declared war on Germany.
2. _____ President of the United States during the American Civil War.
3. _____ Prime Minister during German unification.
4. _____ Confederate commander.
5. _____ Native American chief.

Short Answer Essay:

During the 19th century, a growing number of Americans and Europeans feared that their republican traditions were being steadily eroded by the growth of business monopolies, government corruption, and the violent struggle between capital and labor. In short, there was a lot of anxiety. Yet, in the midst of this turmoil, there were absolutely inspiring speeches presented by men and women. In time, partly because of this inspired rhetoric, future generations would look with nostalgia at the lost century, the last innocent era in modern history. Today, though, in the midst of even greater danger, the art of rhetoric seems to have been lost. No politician can seem to inspire us with their words anymore. Why?

Fill in the blanks with words from the following list:

Chinese Exclusion Act

Lee Chew

Nakahama Manjiro

Pun Chi

William Hooper

1. _____ Japanese American who facilitated understanding between both countries.

2. _____ American sugar cane industrialist in Hawaii who employed many Japanese workers.

3. _____ Asian-American immigrant.

4. _____ Anti-Chinese immigration law at the end of the 19th century.

5. _____ Chinese statesmen who wrote a critical letter to the U. S. Congress.

Short Answer Essay:

After the Civil War, immigrants again began to stream to the United States. Between 1870 and 1900, nearly 12 million immigrants arrived — more foreign-born people than had come to the country in the preceding 70 years. During the 1870s and 1880s, the majority came from Germany, Ireland, and England — the principal source of immigration before the Civil War. Even so, a relatively large group of Chinese immigrated to the United States between the start of the California gold rush in 1849 and 1882, when federal law stopped their immigration. Why?

Fill in the blanks with words from the following list:

Imperialism

Nation building

Nationalism

Romanticism

Völkisch Movement

1. _____ A movement that celebrates the peculiarities and specialness of a geographical area.

2. _____ A movement where a country seeks to colonize or control, or both, other areas of the world.

3. _____ When a nation seeks to "help" another country build its economy, government, and society.

4. _____ A world view that celebrates the subjective and individualism. Gothic Romance: A romantic, dark, sometimes horrible theme that emerges at the end of the 19th century.

5. _____ A folk, indigenous national movement.

Short Answer Essay:

Respond to this blog:

The way many Americans treat the concept of culture, flag, nation — well, borders on idolatry . . . soldiers and draftees are morally obliged to obey orders, and civilians are urged to support the war effort lest they be accused of a bevy of abuses ranging from disloyalty to treason. We see this quite clearly in the ongoing debate today. But it's wrong. It is certainly a necessary condition that the secular leadership evaluates the just war conditions, but it is not a sufficient one. The judgment could be wrong, immoral.

Were soldiers in Nazi Germany obliged to obey orders? Was the German population obliged to support the war effort? Of course not! And the Nuremberg trials concurred; stating clearly that the "following orders" defense was invalid.

Where am I going with this? In earlier days, before the Enlightenment and the rise of the nation state, nationalism, at least as understood today, was non-existent. The ruler was regarded as having a divine mandate to rule, but this was contingent upon the ruler supporting the common good. There was never any obligation to support tyrants. Of course, the environment was very different, during a time when borders were in constant flux, and when there was no real concept of a "state" demanding allegiance. Loyalties were of a local nature. But the rise of nationalism changed the equation, as (absent any notion of the divine) the state itself became an end in itself. It is by no accident that many trace the birth of modern nationalism to the French Revolution. As Christianity waned, secular mythologies and ideologies arose to take its place, and those ideologies often glorified country. In its extreme forms, this ideology quickly shifted into the venomous pseudo-religions that so marked the 20th century. Even its more benign forms (such as in the United States) it is, in its essence, an artificial concept prone to corruption.

Perhaps we need to reassess nationalism. The ruler in a modern democracy is obliged to protect the common good, chiefly to protecting basic human rights. Borders are necessary to establish administrative boundaries. But should these boundaries be accorded a mystical quality of their own? I don't think so.

http://reasons-and-opinions.blogspot.com/2007/01/problem-with-nationalism.html

Fill in the blanks with words from the following list:

Boss Tweed

D. L. Moody

Great Chicago Fire

Industrial Expansion

Tenement housing

1. _____ After the American Civil War, a significant industrial expansion.
2. _____ Urban housing where individuals lived in adjoining apartments.
3. _____ A dishonest, powerful 19th-century New York City politician.
4. _____ Fire that destroyed most of Chicago.
5. _____ Evangelist with an outreach in Chicago.

Short Answer Essay:

No one denies that 19th-century cities were awful places for the poor to live. However, urbanization seemed to be inevitable. Speculate upon how some of the problems of 19th-century urbanization could have been avoided.

Fill in the blanks with words from the following list:

American Missionary Association

Collar starcher

Homeschool

Iron molder

Miner's asthma

1. _____ The American Missionary Association (AMA) was a Protestant-based abolitionist group founded on September 3, 1846, in Albany, New York.

2. _____ A euphemism for black lung disease.

3. _____ One who worked with laundry for a living.

4. _____ One skilled in metalworking.

5. _____ An educational methodology where parents have the role of educator.

Short Answer Essay:

Who would you rather be: the African-American lady, the coal miner, the collar starcher, or the college professor's wife?

Answer Key

Discussion Question Answer Key

Chapter 1

Lesson 1

By any standards, Western Europe was at a new apex of growth. Economically, Europe was in great shape. Apparently the Plague was behind them. Society was transformed by new opportunities: food surpluses and increased populations, revitalized trade, new towns, more affordable (but still very expensive) exotic spices from the Orient, and, thanks to the Wall Street tycoons of the 16th century — the Venetians — a robust European economy based on hard species emerged. The Church wasn't doing half bad either. The church developed the first unified system of law and administration in the medieval age. Every European felt good about that. At the same time, the Crusades had whet everyone's appetite to share the Gospel in strange, new mission fields. Finally, there were advances in ship construction (bigger, faster, and sturdier) and there were new navigation aids.

Lesson 2

The Norse Greenlanders clung to many traditions of Christian Europe. They appeared to be like any European community.

Lesson 3

My in-laws, immigrants from Scotland, told me about a missionary from their church in Scotland who shared Christ with Pastor Cho in South Korea, who, today is the pastor of the largest church in the world. Yet, no one has heard of their friend! They don't even know his name! Answers will vary.

Lesson 4

This is a difficult question. Christopher was a very committed Christian and his views were no better or worse than any other 15th-century European. It still is wrong to exploit people for profit alone.

Lesson 5

The caravel of the 15th and 16th centuries was a magnificent technological feat. Ship captains could venture miles away from shore and return without any problem whatsoever. Of course, even the sturdiest and fastest ship needed to be steered to a desired location. Ingenious technicians designed just what the doctor ordered. One of the earliest man-made navigation tools was the mariner's compass, an early form of the magnetic compass (c.13th century). Much more valuable, at the time, was the invention of the lead line (c.13th century), which was a tool for measuring the depth of water and the nature of the bottom. This line was weighted with lead and had graduated markings to determine sea depth. The lead was coated with wax to bring up samples of the bottom. Also, the astrolabe, which had been around for centuries, was refined to even more accurately determine the longitude and latitude of a ship's location.

Chapter 2

Lesson 1

Native Americans were a very diverse people. The people north of Mexico lived in more than 350 distinct groups, spoke more than 250 different languages, and had their own political structure, kinship systems, and economies. In fact, the differences between these Native American tribes were greater than their similarities. These divisions would have fateful consequences for the future, permitting the European colonizers to play one group against others. In short, by 1492, there were deeply rooted historic conflicts and vulnerabilities that European colonizers would exploit. In the Southwest, many conflicts arose over control of the arid region's scarce resources. Isolated villages were vulnerable to attacks from marauding bands of Apaches and Arapaho. All Native peoples were vulnerable to technologically advanced Spanish invaders. The Europeans played warring tribes against each other. For instance, the Algonquians fought the Iroquois; the Dakota Sioux were mortal enemies of the Crow. In the short run, Native Americans killed more Native Americans than the Europeans killed (except by disease).

Lesson 2

While the differences in Native American cultures were profound and significant, all Native Americans shared certain social tendencies. While many differences and variations existed, there were also uniformities of organization, subsistence, technology, and belief that made them more alike with each other than any one of them was to civilizations of the Old World. While Native Americans had fierce rivalries, socially, they were very similar. Certainly the differences among Native peoples were not as pronounced as those among European countries. As all ancient people groups, most of the differences between Native peoples were related to food gathering. Some people groups were farmers exclusively; some were strictly nomadic food gatherers. The vast majority were both. Unlike other ancient people groups, the Native Americans never developed a commercial industry or class. There was a priestly class, but it was never large and, while it had more of a social impact than the most ambitious European religious clergy group, was not a significant economic player in Native American society. In Europe there were differences among nations too, but these were social and economic differences. European society had developed beyond tension between agrarian and nomadic issues. Now Europe was a continent full of political entities inching relentlessly toward nationalism that would never appear in tribal-based Native American peoples.

Lesson 3

The Native American penchant to live in large kinship groups, many times in the same house, was a great advantage for the first 50 years of European invasion and subsequent colonization, and, almost immediately, was copied. Native American kinship systems were very complicated with unwritten regulations, or traditions would be a better word, governing marriages, relations with in-laws, and residence after marriage. In patrilineal societies, like the Cheyenne, land use rights and membership in the political system originated with the father. In matrilineal societies, like the Pueblo of the Southwest, membership in the group was determined by the mother's family identity. This worked out very well in Native American families. The young people learned critical parenting stills in the first important years after babies were born. There is evidence that the fatality rate among Native American children, age 1–5, was much lower than among other cultures, including Europeans.

Lesson 4

Native American people normally had a strong, tertiary leader who was not unlike the European king or queen. While the European monarch was hereditary, regardless of the ability of the sovereign, Native chiefs were chosen for their bravery, acumen, and élan, not because their father was chief.

Lesson 5

Many, if not most, nations in the world exhibit some form of ethnocentrism. This is especially true of some of the Germanic peoples, but exists all over Europe. Likewise, in Iraq, some people groups are considered inferior.

Chapter 3

Lesson 1

Although far superior in material quality to earlier maps, the maps of the Renaissance were in many ways inferior. Imaginary continents and islands were drawn to fill in extensive blank areas. The unexplored interiors of known land areas were covered with fanciful detail. Borders were decorated with pretentious artwork. The latitudes of Renaissance maps were generally accurate, but the distorted shapes of some coastlines show that longitudes were not.

Lesson 2

The economic advantages of a Northwest Passage outweighed all hardship and expense.

Lesson 3

1. Four hundred years ago most of the people who lived in Europe thought that the earth was flat. That is untrue and surely Shaw knew it. No scientist in 1400 thought that the world was flat and surely no historian in 1900 thought otherwise. One wonders if he was increasing his readership by creating a fanciful history.

2. Here they made maps and charts, and talked with one another about the strange lands they thought might be found far out in that mysterious body of water they so dreaded and feared. It is probable that they had heard some accounts of the voyages of other navigators on this wonderful sea, and the beliefs about land beyond. Again, this is speculation and opinion. Does Shaw have any written source that he can offer?

Lesson 4

Ultimately the legitimacy of a secondary source is tied to its primary source. Also, the motivation and training of the historian matters a great deal too. If a source is advancing a certain agenda, then he surely will not hesitate to put a certain slant on a historical fact! For instance, it is amazing how biased and indurate some secondary accounts of events by present day media can be.

Lesson 5

Perhaps it has never ended but, practically speaking, it ended when the Antarctica and North Pole were explored in the 1950s.

Chapter 4

Lesson 1

Europeans loved to stereotype the Native Americans. Many Europeans regarded the Native Americans as immoral and free of all of civilization's restraints. They were wild men and women and certainly inferior to Europeans. Surprisingly, there was a contradictory stereotype too. According to this stereotype, the Native Americans embodied innocence and freedom, lacking private property, yet possessing health and eternal youth. Another favorite stereotype was the wise Native American who assists whites in their plans to civilize the wilderness. But if some Europeans regarded Native Americans with fascination, most looked at them with fear. The "bloodthirsty savage" who stood in the way of progress and civilization was the stereotype of choice.

Lesson 2

The French and the Native Americans they encountered reached a different kind of accommodation. France's New World empire was based largely on trade. In 1504, French fishermen sailed into the Gulf of St. Lawrence, looking for cod. Gradually, the French realized that they could increase their profits by trading with the Native Americans for furs. In exchange, French traders supplied Native Americans with clothing, weapons, and other trade goods. In fact, by 1700, a thousand ships a year were engaged in the fur trade along the St. Lawrence River and the interior, where the French constructed forts, missions, and trading posts. It was a hugely profitable business for the French.

Lesson 3

Unlike the French and Spanish, the English created self-sustaining settler colonies, populated with immigrants. And this meant owning land and displacing the indigenous inhabitants.

Lesson 4

England, France, the Netherlands, and Spain all competed over trade with the Native Americans. In the long run the English won; everyone else lost. But the big losers were the Native Americans. Competition over furs, skins, and other trading goods had many destructive effects on Native Americans. It made Native Americans increasingly dependent on European manufactured goods and firearms. The trade also killed animals that provided a major part of the hunting and gathering economy. Traders spread disease; alcohol debilitated whole tribes. Above all, competition over trade encouraged intertribal warfare and thus undermined the Native Americans' ability to resist.

Lesson 5

This is instructive. Increasingly the Lewis Wetzels, both in the European community and in the Native American community, affected the nature of European and Native American relations that emerged in the 18th and 19th centuries. There was quite simply, no middle ground among these people groups. Everything was radicalized.

Chapter 5

Lesson 1

Feudalism remained much longer in Russia because, actually, it worked! While the serfs (peasants) were poor, some desperately, they at least mostly were eating well. They were able to farm the vast steppes that are a part of Russia. I am not justifying feudalism, but in a huge nation like Russia, it worked. At the same time, Peter the Great, and some industrialists, saw that Russia had to modernize its society, especially its army, or it would forever be a second-rate power.

Lesson 2

Nationalism in places like Sweden helped the growing middle class gain influence that it so desperately needed to empower the young Swedish nation. The problem is, unfortunately, nationalism often stimulates autocratic and despotic governments. Napoleon followed the French Revolution. Hitler followed the Weimar Republic. Why? Nationalism encourages a romantic patriotism that allows, even encourages, the formation of a strong, central government.

Lesson 3

Europe was powered, and would be powered for two centuries, by a farm economy. Using bigger fields or working longer may have improved productivity up to a point, but soon it would have met a ceiling: a human being cannot work more than 12 hours in the fields. Accumulating capital in agriculture is very difficult. This was accomplished by selling surplus food in the urban markets. Even the smallest European farm was producing a surplus that was ending up in urban marketplaces and generating a growing amount of income. This was called the commercialization of one's surplus. Thus, the humble farmer's market, in 1600, was probably the richest part of town. So, what caused growth in this tumultuous era? Wealth emerged in labor. The European laborer was dexterous, diligent, and productive. And his productivity was increasing. For example, an investor could hire 56 men to travel to Virginia or Maryland and grow tobacco and, given the nature of European labor, there was a very good chance that the laborers would grow a bumper crop of tobacco and the investors would make a huge profit. Of course these workers, indentured servants, were only obligated to work for the "company" for a few years, but there was a seemingly endless supply of labor and new cultivatable land.

Lesson 4

Inevitably, agrarian prosperity engenders urban growth. A great example is Italy. City-states prospered. The prosperity, though, was based on the commercial surpluses of farmers. Sooner or later, premodern economies reached their limit, weakened, and collapsed. The increased agricultural productivity would allow population to grow, but at one point a production setback would create food shortage, weaken people's bodies, and many of them would die due to malnutrition. This would lead markets to retract. Traders and artisans lost confidence in their food providers. This confidence might quickly cause a once-prosperous farmer to stay home on Saturday. When he did this, he did not sell his surpluses, and he did not buy the artisan products. In economic terms this means that the linkage between two industries was broken. Both suffered. The maintenance of this fragile relationship assured premodern European prosperity. Nonetheless, the premodern economy did very well and, thanks to overseas expansion, became quite multinational and promised a firm base full of available capital for the Industrial Revolution that was just around the corner.

Lesson 5

An international war is fought between two or more states. At the simplest level it is a conflict between two nations. The French and Indian War, really an Anglo-French war, is an example. Inevitably international wars involve coalitions of allied nations fighting each other. This happened, but rarely. When it did, it rarely resulted in total war. Total war implied the complete mobilization of a society, its citizens, and its industries to provide the military means to wage war. Again, very few wars required total mobilization. No war was fought like that until the Napoleonic Wars of the 19th century.

Chapter 6

Lesson 1

Modern historians have accepted the term Renaissance as a convenient label for this exciting age of intellectual and artistic revival, which continued through the sixteenth century. But since the Renaissance had deep roots in the Middle Ages, which also made rich contributions to civilization, in what ways can the Renaissance be said to signify a "rebirth"? Of course there are some old grouches, like myself, who have a few problems with the Renaissance. For one thing,

I miss the Christ-centered art and philosophy that was replaced by art and philosophy replete with humanism and self-centeredness. Next, the author does not wish to see the Church vilified. The Church, if anything, encouraged, and more than that, paid for the Renaissance! Who do you think paid Michelangelo to do the Sistine Chapel? The philosopher Hobbes laconically stated that the Church was nothing more than the ghost of the dead Roman Empire.

Lesson 2

Inevitably a grievance mentality leads to a myopic vision of the world — unforgivingness and stale culture. The institution, the movement, infests too much time and talent denigrating the competing or dominant culture, and not enough time building its own culture.

Lesson 3

Italy had wealth. The city-states were floating in profits from the Crusades and the spice trade of previous centuries. Italy had a language. All these conspired to make Italy the leader in the nascent Renaissance.

Lesson 4

Answers will vary. Candidates might be the iPod or iPhone.

Lesson 5

To celebrate the value and strength of mankind in any setting is to invite the same consideration in all.

Chapter 7

Lesson 1

The classical concept of beaux-arts, a term that was coined in France during the 18th century, was reclaimed. The arts of the beautiful were separated from the arts of the useful because of the belief that the fine arts had a special quality: they served to give pleasure to an audience. The type of pleasure was called aesthetic, and it referred to the satisfaction given to the individual or group solely from perceiving — seeing or hearing — a work of art.

Lesson 2

The art of the ancient Greeks is called classical art. Greek art owes its lasting influence to its simplicity and reasonableness, its humanity, and its sheer beauty.

They were interested chiefly in portraying gods, however, since mankind was never perfect. What they were trying to portray was ideal beauty rather than any particular person. Today we have statues of George Washington or Abraham Lincoln. The Greeks would never think of doing that. Their best sculptures achieved almost godlike perfection in their calm, ordered beauty. It was about a type of person, not a specific person.

Lesson 3
Answers will vary.

Lesson 4
For its age, the baroque style was modern art. Taken literally, the term means "irregular" and is applied generally to the dynamic and undisciplined artistic creativity of the seventeenth century. My favorite is Rembrandt van Rijn (1606—1669). While reflecting the common characteristics of his school, he produced works so ordinary and human that they not only expressed Dutch cultural values but also transcended them. As one critic explains, "His canvasses show tremendous sensitivity, depicting almost every human emotion except pure joy." Rembrandt was the master of chiaroscuro. This was an artistic strategy that emphasized falling light on subjects.

Lesson 5
1. It restored the Broken Unity of History. When Christianity entered the ancient Greco-Roman world, war declared itself at once between the new religion and classical culture, especially between it and Hellenism. 2. It reformed Education. 3. It inspired humanity with a new spirit, a spirit destined in time to make things new in all realms, — in the realm of religion, of politics, of literature, of art, of science, of invention, of industry.

Chapter 8

Lesson 1
Historians look in vain for socio-political reasons for the Reformation. It was absolutely, and definitively, a religious revolution. The Reformation started with a German Monk, Martin Luther. The truth is, the common people sought a more personal, spiritual, and immediate kind of religion — something that would touch them directly, in the heart more than the Roman Catholic Church. The premodern Renaissance world promised more than the extant structures, especially the Church, could meet. To some of us, too, it seems that the Holy Spirit prompted Martin Luther to reclaim something that seemed to have been lost.

Lesson 2
Justification by faith and the priesthood of all believers are the two most important theological issues.

Lesson 3
Middle East conflicts; conflicts in Bosnia.

Lesson 4
The Roman Catholic leadership underestimated the extent of the Reformation at first, considering it just another schism. They learned soon enough that they were wrong. They convened a group of scholars and clergy to a council meeting, the Council of Trent, to launch a vigorous counterattack. From 1545 to 1563 the Council of Trent both corrected church abuses and affirmed orthodoxy. The truth is, the Council of Trent was partly successful. The ardor of some potential dissenters was cooled. By the close of the 16th century the Roman Catholic Church had regained half of the lands it had lost to Protestantism.

Lesson 5
De Sales states that if one argues from the Protestant position, who determines what the Scripture means that interprets the other Scripture in question. "The Scriptures," says S. Jerome, "consist not in the reading but in the understanding:" that is, faith is not in the knowing the words but the sense. And it is here that I think I have thoroughly proved that we have need of another rule for our faith, besides the rule of Holy Scripture. "If the world last long" said Luther once by good hap "it will be again necessary, on account of the different interpretations of Scripture which now exist, that to preserve the unity of the faith we should receive the Councils and decrees and fly to them for refuge." He acknowledges that formerly they were received, and that afterwards they will have to be. "I have dwelt on this at length, but when it is well understood, we have no small means of determining a most holy deliberation.

I say as much of Traditions; for if each one will bring forward Traditions, and we have no judge on earth to make in the last resort the difference between those which are to be received and those which are not, where, I pray you, shall we be? We have clear examples. Calvin finds that the Apocalypse is to be received, Luther denies it; the same with the Epistle of S. James. Who shall reform these opinions of the reformers? Either the one or the other is ill formed, who shall put it right? Here is a second necessity which we have of another rule besides the Word of God.

This author, personally, finds the Protestant interpretation persuasive. It seems to me that De Sales is just dancing around the central question: Who is the final authority on Scriptural interpretations: man or God? I love, however, and respect, fellow Roman Catholic believers and their views on the subject.

Chapter 9

Lesson 1

The essential characteristic of all government, whatever its form, is authority. There must in every instance be, on the one hand, governors, and, on the other, those who are governed. And the authority of governors, directly or indirectly, rests in all cases ultimately on force. Government, in its last analysis, is organized force. Not necessarily or invariably organized armed force, but the will of a few men, of many men, or of a community prepared by organization to realize its own purposes with reference to the common affairs of the community. Organized, that is, to rule, to dominate. The machinery of government necessary to such an organization consists of instrumentalities fitted to enforce in the conduct of the common affairs of a community the will of the sovereign men: the sovereign minority, or the sovereign majority (Wilson).

Lesson 2

The key to constitutional democracy and the emerging was facilitated by prosperity that more or less blessed all classes (rich and poor, urban and rural). Concentration of power in any one office or individual was limited by interaction of classes. Their differences were accented by their separate interests and by their indirect exercise of power, outside of government and often outside of the law itself. A lot of informal alliances and propitious compromises occurred in pubs and boarding houses in both countries. These later became political parties and factions.

Lesson 3

Absolute monarchy was not exactly new in Europe. It wasn't new anywhere. Absolutism was a government that made all the choices for everyone. One must not think that absolutism was an unpopular government. On the contrary, the favorite choice was an absolute monarchy. Some Europeans preferred the predictability and order of tyranny to the tentativeness of democracy. Since the late medieval period, rulers had been slowly centralizing their authority at the expense of feudal nobles and the church. In the sixteenth and early seventeenth centuries, however, the Reformation retarded progress somewhat. After the Peace of Westphalia, which ended the Thirty Years' War, absolutism rapidly gained popularity because it promised to restore order and security. Europeans had had enough of 30-year wars!

Lesson 4

To Hobbes power, human power, raw unadulterated power, was the currency of the land. To Hobbes, everything else was only a metaphor of what was real. Men in a state of nature, that is a state without civil government, are in a war of all against all in which life is hardly worth living. The way out of this desperate state was to make a social contract and establish the state to keep peace and order. The state then, not the individual, was the most important consideration in political power. The purposes of God, as outlined in Scripture, were not important.

Lesson 5

Christians favor, of course, a form of moral absolutism. Sin is always wrong, no matter what the circumstances or motivation. Hobbes' version of moral absolutism is an ethical view that certain actions are absolutely right or wrong, regardless of other contexts such as their consequences or the intentions behind them. Hobbes brand of absolutism is that things are right because they can be done, because the doer is powerful enough to do them. Not because they are in fact right or wrong based on the Word of God. At the same time, Christians must remember the axiom: never overcome evil with evil, even if the thing that overcomes the evil thing is right. We must not kill pro-choice people even though they are wrong! World War II German Christians must not murder Jewish people even though it is legal to do so, even though it is encouraged.

Chapter 10

Lesson 1

New discoveries in astronomy, physics, chemistry, and even biology strongly suggested that nature, from the smallest particle to the most distant stars, was an interlocking mechanism of harmoniously working parts. Not that most, if any, gave up their faith in God. On the contrary, what a God they served if He had so deliberately and completely created a universe like this! No, science invited people to draw closer to God. It stimulated and confirmed the faith of people. This is not the invective science that emerged in the 19th century, specifically, that science related to evolution. No, this was science that talked about the stars and blood circulation and other amazing things. Here, apparently, was the simple answer to an everlasting search for certainty and the immediate origin of optimistic hopes for humanity.

Lesson 2

Inductive reasoning is a kind of reasoning that constructs or evaluates propositions that are abstractions of observations of individual instances of members of the same class. It is commonly construed as a form of reasoning that makes generalizations based on empirical evidence. Deductive reason is developed through logical, rhetorical passageways that data may have prompted, or not.

Lesson 3

Time stopped for Joshua, and it ran backward for Hezekiah (2 Kings 20:9–11).

God may have temporarily reversed the earth's rotation, including all its inhabitants, or the miracle in Hezekiah's day could have been local instead of worldwide. The latter view is supported by 2 Chronicles 32:31, which describes envoys who traveled to the land where the miracle occurred.

Lesson 4

Advances in technology, in particular, gave European nations a significant edge over other nations and culture. Scientific and economic superiority harnessed to efficient state structures provided the strength for the European expansion and domination. Europeans improved the cannon, the rifle, and almost every other war instrument in existence. Europeans, and Western people in general, have always been good at making war! But these advances in weaponry assured European hegemony in the 16th century.

Lesson 5

Answers will vary.

Chapter 11

Lesson 1

Slavery was immensely valuable. Also there was a lot of prejudice in general against people of another race.

Lesson 2

There were several intertribal wars that supplied ample slaves to be traded. Also, slavery existed in every African nation. Finally, Islamic traders set up a very effective trade system that brought the "product" quickly and safely.

Lesson 3

The main stimulus of slave trade was Islam. The spread of Islam from Arabia into Africa after the religion's founding in the 7th century AD affected the practice of slavery and slave trading in West, Central, and East Africa. Arabs were good at it. They knew how to run the business end of slavery.

Lesson 4

West and West Central African states willingly supplied the Europeans with African slaves for export across the Atlantic. Africans tended to live longer on the tropical plantations of the New World than did European laborers (who eventually won their freedom) and Native Americans (who were undependable). Also, enslaved men and women from Africa were relatively inexpensive and could be owned by almost any colonist. Therefore, African slaves became the primary source of New World plantation labor. Slaves were affordable and available. The Africans who facilitated and benefited from the Atlantic slave trade were political and commercial elites, far more erudite and sophisticated than their European customers. The Africans were shrewd and skillful businessmen. One should not suppose that African traders were naïve, stupid entrepreneurs as European buyers characterized them. They had been doing business in the slave trade for centuries. In short, slave trading was the most profitable industry for about 400 years. The truth is, slavery enriched everyone. The slave trader sold the slave to the European customer for the equivalent of four or five dollars. The European owner would sell the same slave to a West Indian farmer for $250. The West Indian farmer would grow sugar cane with virtually no labor costs and make more profit. One slave could generate a veritable fortune in the commercial cycle.

Lesson 5

The PBS "Terrible Transformation" states, "For weeks, months, sometimes as long as a year, they waited in the dungeons of the slave factories scattered along Africa's western coast. They had already made the long, difficult journey from Africa's interior — but just barely. Out of the roughly 20 million who were taken from their homes and sold into slavery, half didn't complete the journey to the African coast, most of those dying along the way. And the worst was yet to come. The captives were about to embark on the infamous Middle Passage, so called because it was the middle leg of a three-part voyage — a voyage that began and ended in Europe. The first leg of the voyage carried a cargo that often included iron, cloth, brandy, firearms, and gunpowder. Upon landing on Africa's 'slave coast,' the cargo was exchanged for Africans. Fully loaded with its human cargo, the ship set sail for the Americas, where the slaves were exchanged for sugar, tobacco, or some other product. The final leg brought the ship back to Europe." http://www.pbs.org/wgbh/aia/part1/1p277.html

Chapter 12

Lesson 1

It was cheap, available labor.

Lesson 2

Slavery in the New World was partly based on racial distinctions. Slavery was permanent. It was the labor force for a high profit economy. Slavery was the lowest status in society.

Lesson 3

Slave religious and cultural traditions played a vital role in enabling slaves to survive the misery of life under slavery. A historian explains, "Many slaves drew on African customs when they buried their dead. Conjurors adapted and blended African religious rites that made use of herbs and supernatural powers. Slaves also perpetuated a rich tradition of West and Central African parables, proverbs, verbal games, and legends. They also retained in their folklore certain central figures. Cunning tricksters, often represented as tortoises, spiders, or rabbits, outwitted their more powerful enemies. Through folklore, slaves also sustained a sense of separate identity and conveyed valuable lessons to their children. Among the most popular folktales were animal trickster stories, like the Brer Rabbit tales, derived from similar African stories, which told of powerless creatures who achieved their will through wit and guile, not power and authority."

Lesson 4

I am not sure. But slaves were far from home, many established families, and it was simply impossible to organize large rebellions.

Lesson 5

Latin America was predominantly a Roman Catholic area. The Roman Catholic Church opposed slavery. Slaves were a larger percentage of the population in Latin America. Probably the greatest difference, however, between Latin American slavery and United States slavery, was toleration for race mixing. It simply was not tolerated in the United States. In fact, it was illegal in every state.

Chapter 13

Lesson 1

Rienzi was instrumental in bringing the papacy back from France to be headquartered in Rome.

Lesson 2

It could not meet the English need for pomp and ritual. "It is meritorious to insist on forms; Religion and all else naturally clothes itself in forms. Everywhere the formed world is the only habitable one. The naked formlessness of Puritanism is not the thing I praise in the Puritans;

it is the thing I pity — praising only the spirit which had rendered that inevitable! All substances clothe themselves in forms: but there are suitable true forms, and then there are untrue unsuitable. As the briefest definition, one might say, Forms which grow round a substance, if we rightly understand that, will correspond to the real nature and purport of it, will be true, good; forms which are consciously put round a substance, bad. I invite you to reflect on this. It distinguishes true from false in Ceremonial Form, earnest solemnity from empty pageant, in all human things."

Lesson 3

Jacobites were supporters of James II, but, over the years, Jacobites became any group of people who were dissatisfied with the regime and sought to overthrow it.

Lesson 4

The American Revolution touched off an "age of revolution." Its example helped inspire revolutions across the entire western world. During the late 1700s and early 1800s, revolutions and popular uprisings erupted from the Ural Mountains in Russia to the Andes Mountains in South America: in Greece, Ireland, Italy, Mexico, Poland, Switzerland, and in many other countries. In Haiti, for the first time in history, slaves succeeded in winning their independence by force of arms. These revolutions, more or less, referenced the American Revolution. (Timothy Hall, World History, NY: Penguin Group, 2008, pp. 215 ff). The American Revolution was fought for popular sovereignty, the novel idea that all governments existed for the benefit of the governed. Whenever a government violated the peoples' fundamental rights, they had the right to change or overthrow it.

Lesson 5

Answers will vary.

Chapter 14

Lesson 1

My favorites are Romans 8 and Ephesians 1. I also like to memorize and pray the entire Book of James.

Lesson 2

Anabaptists are the originators of the "free church." Today they are called Mennonites. Separation of church and state was an unthinkable and radical notion when it was introduced by the Anabaptists. Their views were universally perceived as causing anarchy.

Lesson 3

Few people, however, have been as frequently subjected to caricature and ridicule. The journalist H.L. Mencken defined Puritanism as "the haunting fear that someone, somewhere, might be happy." G. K. Chesterton in his *Short History of England* (1917) was not very flattering in his assessment of Puritanism either. The Puritans have came to symbolize every cultural characteristic that "modern" Americans despise. The Puritans were often dismissed as rigid religious bigots who were miserable and tried to make everyone around them miserable. The Puritans inevitably are presented as religious bigots and prudish people. Nothing could be more untrue.

Lesson 4

These two historians agree. Mintz, though, emphasizes the sociological, cultural impact of this important revival. Dienstberger emphasizes the religious and theological changes in American society.

Lesson 5

When the Great Awakening started, the only thing the thirteen colonies had in common was that they were loosely tied to the English crown. At the close the most noteworthy feature of the event was that it was the first national experience in American history. From New England to Georgia an intercolonial visitation by the Holy Spirit had touched America. In every colony a new enthusiasm for Christianity appeared. The awakening even reached over denominational lines; churches cooperated with each other in a spirit of Christian brotherhood. When it was over, no one doubted that God had moved across America.

Chapter 15

Lesson 1

2 Timothy 2:16 All Scripture is God-breathed and is useful for teaching, rebuking, correcting and training in righteousness. The Holy Spirit, not humans, are the true authors of the Word of God. The Bible alone is the only authority that one may use to judge the veracity of a text.

Lesson 2

The biblical canon is a list of books considered to be authoritative as scripture by orthodox (or the majority) of Christians. It is amazing how the Holy Spirit created this anointed list — we call it the Bible — in one generation by bringing unanimity among divergent Christian groups.

Lesson 3

In defense of the Roman Catholic Church, at the end of the Middle Ages, the Church felt threatened by teachings and positions that encouraged unorthodoxy. The Church issued this edict in 1399: " . . . that none . . . presume to preach openly or privily, without the license of the diocesan of the same place first required and obtained, curates in their own churches and persons hitherto privileged, and other of the Canon Law granted, only except; nor that none from henceforth anything preach, hold, teach, or instruct openly or privily, or make or write any book contrary to the catholic faith or determination of the Holy Church, nor of such sect and wicked doctrines and opinions shall make any conventicles, or in any wise hold or exercise schools; and also that none from henceforth in any wise favor such preacher or maker of any such and like conventicles, or persons holding or exercising schools, or making or writing such books, or so teaching, informing, or exciting the people, nor any of them maintain or in any wise sustain, and that all and singular having such books or any writings of such wicked doctrine and opinions, shall really with effect deliver or cause to be delivered all such books and writings to the diocesan of the same place within forty days from the time of the proclamation of this ordinance and statute." The Roman Catholic Church recognized the power of the written word and was determined to contain its influence on the common man. To a Church that put such stock on tradition and ecclesiology, such measures made a great deal of sense.

Lesson 4

The Puritans and the Pilgrims fled the religious persecution of England to cross the Atlantic and start a new free nation in America. They took with them their Geneva Bibles and rejected the King James Bible. America was founded upon the Geneva Bible, not the King James Bible. Initially the King James Bible was perceived as a pro–Church of England version and the Puritan and Pilgrim reformers would have nothing to do with it.

Lesson 5

The author agrees with historians like Perry Miller who argued persuasively that one cannot understand American history without understanding its religious history.

Chapter 16

Lesson 1

The concept of covenant, so important to Puritanism, was not new. The notion that a people group would found a commonwealth based entirely, specifically on the Word of God was new except for in the nation of Israel.

Lesson 2

The New England Confederation was a loose confederation, each colony retaining its home government as before. The main object in uniting was to protect themselves from their common enemies — from the Native Americans, from the Dutch on the west, the French on the north, and even from England, which was torn apart in a civil war. Some historians see this union as nothing more than a business arrangement, but it surely presaged later colonial attempts at union. At the same time, it was a very political, as well as business, arrangement. The colonies used this as a basis of cooperation during the French and Native American War as well as the subsequent Revolution.

Lesson 3

The New England Confederation was a loose confederation, each colony retaining its home government as before. The main object in uniting was to protect themselves from their common enemies — from the Native Americans, from the Dutch on the west, the French on the north, and even from England, which was torn apart in a civil war. Some historians see this union as nothing more than a business arrangement, but it surely presaged later colonial attempts at union. At the same time, it was a very political, as well as business, arrangement. The colonies used this as a basis of cooperation during the French and Native American War as well as the subsequent Revolution.

Lesson 4

Governor Andros was only partially able to remove colonial independence. But the ancient independence was gone. The laws were again to be made and the taxes levied by a legislature elected by the people; but every act must henceforth be sent to England for royal approval; and henceforth the governor, his deputy, and secretary were to be appointments of the Crown. The new charter also opened the door of citizenship, requiring a property test, but no longer a religious test. This feature destroyed forever that intimate union of Church and State that had characterized the first generation in Massachusetts Bay. The Church and State were still united, but the Puritan hierarchy had full control and the assembly rendered it unlike any other American charter. From this cause Massachusetts is often placed in a class by itself as a semi-royal colony.

Lesson 5

Answers will vary.

Chapter 17

Lesson 1

This reader finds him very reliable. He both respects the Native Americans (calls them by name not "savages") and his fair treatment of the French. Plus, he admits that the English were cowards too: "the Colonel with men behaved themselves cowardly for some minutes but [were] overpowered by such a vast company their number suppose to consist of 2500 men compelling Colonel with his 600 to fight and upon a retreat until they came to the Fort at the Lake."

Lesson 2

The young people were apostate, but there was a great revival. "Just after my Grandfather's Death, it seemed to be a time of extraordinary Dullness in Religion: Licentiousness for some Years greatly prevailed among the Youth of the Town; they were many of them very much addicted to Night-walking, and frequently the Tavern, and lewd Practices, wherein some, by their Example, exceedingly corrupted others. It was their Manner very frequently to get together, in Conventions of both Sexes, for Mirth and Jollity, which they called Frolicks; and they would often spend the greater part of the Night in them, without regard to any Order in the Families they belonged to: and indeed Family-Government did too much fail in the Town. It was become very customary with many of our young People, to be Indecent in their Carriage at Meetin . . . ; the young People declared themselves convinced by what they had heard from the Pulpit, and were willing of themselves to comply with the Counsel that had been given: and it was immediately, and, I suppose, almost universally complied with; and there was a thorough Reformation of these Disorders thenceforward, which has continued ever since. . . Presently upon this, a great and earnest Concern about the great Things of Religion, and the eternal World, became universal in all Parts of the Town, and among Persons of all Ages. . ."

Lesson 3

"During the voyage there is on board these ships terrible misery, stench, fumes, horror, vomiting, many kinds of sea-sickness, fever, dysentery, headache, heat, constipation, boils, scurvy, cancer, mouth-rot, and the like, all of which come from old and sharply salted food and meat, also from very bad and foul water, so that many die miserably. . . . At length, when, after a long and tedious voyage, the ships come in sight of land, so that the promontories can be seen, which the people were so eager and anxious to see, all creep from below on deck to see the land from afar, and they weep for joy, and pray and sing, thanking and praising God. . . . But alas! When the ships have landed at Philadelphia after their long voyage, no one is permitted to leave them, except those who pay for their passage or can give good security. The others, who cannot pay, must remain on board the ships till they are purchased, and are released from the ships by their purchasers. The sick always fare the worst, for the healthy are naturally preferred and purchased first. And so the sick and wretched must often remain on board in front of the city for two or three weeks, and frequently die; whereas many a one, if he could pay his debt and were permitted to leave the ship immediately, might recover and remain alive. . . ." Many of these poor immigrants would have to experience servitude until their 21st birthdays or seven years. They did this because of the opportunities that America afforded all arriving immigrants.

Lesson 4

The slaves were slaves, many treated poorly. They had been snatched from their own and inflicted to months of horror on ships. There is no justification for the gratuitous violence in NYC in 1741, but neither is there any justification for the inhumane treatment that slaves endured in chattel slavery.

Lesson 5

It is a very hard life! It is full of privation and want. The only consoling fact is that this lady has a loving family and community who shares her life.

Chapter 18

Lesson 1

Adams was not only a great statesman, he was a committed Christian. He understood the biblical injunction to forgive others if one is to be forgiven. At the same time, Adams, encouraged by his wife, refused to allow any bitterness to consume his heart.

Lesson 2

Answers will vary. Most social critics argue persuasively that this generation is one of the most hopeless in history. Interestingly enough, this hopelessness has made us rather sentimental. We have become very sentimental about the past. Even in our most creative creations it is more of the same. Even though he is a loner, a womanizer, he still is a do-gooder spreading George Lucas' version of truth and justice across the land. But God is totally absent. The Star Wars phenomenon is so appealing because it is about the past, not about the future. Luke Skywalker is more like John Wayne than he is like Tom Cruise. To this hopeless generation, history is not sacred; it is merely utilitarian. It is not didactic; it helps make them feel better. The modern psychologist B.F. Skinner, for instance, disdains history and gives M&M's to monkeys. We have no actions — only fate driving us. We are rudderless. The fact is we Christians know, however, that God is in absolute control of history. We need to teach our children to be tirelessly hopeful. We need to make sure that we are not mawkish! We can easily do so by speaking the Truth found in the Word of God in places of deception.

Lesson 3

Franklin was a genuine "rags to riches" story. He truly knew what it was to be poor and how to work hard toward a goal. Also, he was self-educated. He was no John Adams — educated at Harvard — but he brought a strong sense of vision and mission to every task he encountered. He truly was, all of his life, the champion of the common man.

Lesson 4

Alexander Hamilton was a very capable soldier and in March 1777, General George Washington appointed him a lieutenant colonel in the Continental Army and a staff offer to Washington himself. He served with Washington for four years. He was able to lead an army group in the Battle of Yorktown in October 1781. Hamilton's personal life and social position in the new nation took a decisive turn in December 1780, when he married Elizabeth Schuyler, daughter of the wealthy and influential General Philip Schuyler. This connection placed Hamilton in the center of New York society. In 1782, shortly after leaving the army, he was admitted to legal practice in New York and became assistant to the most important lawyer in the colonies, Robert Morris (1734–1806). Before his 30th birthday, then, Hamilton had had a distinguished military career, knew intimately most of the leaders of the American Revolution, was wealthy beyond his dreams, and was recognized as one of the best lawyers in the country.

Lesson 5

Morris certainly was a capable man, but the Constitutional Convention was full of capable men. He was a typical 19th-century Founding Father: principled, hard working, intelligent, and creative.

Chapter 19

Lesson 1

Given the high risk of birth complications and infant death, it is not surprising to learn that pregnancy was surrounded by superstitions. It was widely believed that if a mother looked upon a "horrible specter" or was startled by a loud noise, her child would be disfigured. If a hare jumped in front of her, her child was in danger of suffering a harelip. There was also fear that if the mother looked at the moon, her child might become a lunatic or sleepwalker.

Lesson 2

Parental involvement in courtship was expected because marriage was not merely an emotional relationship between individuals but also a property arrangement among families. A young man was expected to bring land or some other form of property to a marriage while a young woman was expected to bring a dowry worth about half as much.

Lesson 3

Funerals were somber occasions, but also occasions to "witness the resurrection of a loved one." Death was not an ending to most 17th- and 18th-century families; it was a beginning. Life began at conversion and did not end with the cessation of physical life. The first grave markers were wooden, and early grave stones contained words but no designs because the Puritans thought that the Second Commandment prohibited the use of graven images. Elaborate funerals or headstones seemed like idolatry. The original headstones faced east, so that on the morning of the Day of Resurrection, the bodies will respectfully face their loving Father God.

Lesson 4

As science made steady progression and continued to "demystify" nature, art responded in kind. As the 17th century drew to a close, the discoveries of science steadily increased human understanding as well as control of the natural world, and affirmed superiority of human reason. In other words, the human intellect eclipsed faith as the guiding force of civilization. This deeply impacted the 18th-century artistic impulse.

Lesson 5

They had no control over anything. Families were separated. Fathers had to work one place and live

in another. There were incredible pressures on slave families.

Chapter 20

Lesson 1

The Swedes, like the French in the 19th century and the Germans in the 20th century, conquered Russian armies but could not conquer Russia. Ultimately, the Russian vast steppes, and indomitable people, won the wars. Likewise the British won in the North, in the South, and even in the Middle States.

Lesson 2

In the fighting at Blenheim, the Allies lost 4,542 killed and 7,942 wounded, while the French and Bavarians suffered approximately 20,000 killed and wounded as well as 14,190 captured. The Duke of Marlborough's victory at Blenheim ended the French threat to Vienna and removed the aura of invincibility that surrounded the armies of Louis XIV. The battle was a turning point in the War of Spanish Succession, ultimately leading to the Grand Alliance's victory and an end of French hegemony over Europe.

Lesson 3

The Battle of Quebec, on the Plains of Abraham, essentially ended the French and Indian War in England's favor. France's influence in North America essentially disappeared and the resurgent English, and a weak New Spain, remained in North America.

Lesson 4

The Americans used the engagement as propaganda to turn the public opinion to their cause. At the time of the battle, only one third of the population believed in breaking from Britain.

Lesson 5

France was the premier continental power in Europe. This crushing victory, coupled with First Consul Napoleon Bonaparte's victory at the Battle of Marengo on June 14, 1800, ended the War of the Second Coalition. In February 1801, the Austrians signed the Treaty of Lunéville, accepting French control up to the Rhine and the French puppet republics in Italy and the Netherlands. The subsequent Treaty of Amiens between France and Britain began the longest break in the wars of the Napoleonic period.

Chapter 21

Lesson 1
He finds himself aborting unborn children and other disturbing things.

Lesson 2
With the dawn of the 18th century, there was a renewed optimism and hopefulness that was birthed in the crucible of natural rights and liberty. Science, like many of the social sciences, explored and discovered new vistas. One historian explains, "As a result, a new optimism pervaded the age. This optimism had the ultimate effect of changing man's opinions about human history. Instead of viewing human history as the story of the steady decline from the Garden of Eden, men now began to view life as full of promise and hope. In characteristic 18th century language, the dawn of the New Jerusalem seemed to be just around the corner. However, this would be a Jerusalem of this world, not postponed until some life after death."

Lesson 3
What united all Enlightenment thinkers was their common experience of shedding their inherited Christian beliefs. They agreed that Christianity was a supernatural religion. It was wrong. It was unreasonable. Only science, with its predictable, empirical results was the way to truth and happiness.

Lesson 4
18th-century chemist Joseph Priestley did not want to be a chemist at all. He wanted to be a pastor. However, before long, as math and science replaced his faith, the ministry became ancillary to his scientific studies, and then this calling disappeared altogether only to be reborn in a humanist, heretical movement called Unitarianism.

Lesson 5
Using 19th-century technology, on March 13, 1781, William Herschel discovered what he first thought to be a comet, but was later found to be planet Uranus.

Chapter 22

Lesson 1
Some events are so catastrophic, terrible, they may seem like fiction. But this passage rings true. American author Kurt Vonnegut Jr. said, "I write what people think is science fiction. But it is so real that it reads like fiction."

Lesson 2
The Marquis writes "The first is the great number of alliances that French keep up with the Indian Nations. These people, who hardly act except from instinct, love us hitherto a little and fear us a great deal, more than they do the English; but their interest, which some among them begin to understand, is that the strength of the English and French remain nearly equal, so that through the jealousy of these two nations those tribes may live independent of, and draw presents from, both. The second reason of our superiority over the English is, the number of French Canadians who are accustomed to live in the woods like the Indians, and become thereby not only qualified to lead them to fight the English, but to wage war even against these same Indians when necessity obliges."

Lesson 3
Wadsworth says, "Concerning the duties of this relation we may assert a few things. It is their duty to dwell together with one another. Surely they should dwell together; if one house cannot hold them, surely they are not affected to each other as they should be. They should have a very great and tender love and affection to one another. This is plainly commanded by God. This duty of love is mutual; it should be performed by each, to each of them. When, therefore, they quarrel or disagree, then they do the Devil's work; he is pleased at it, glad of it. But such contention provokes God; it dishonors Him; it is a vile example before inferiors in the family; it tends to prevent family prayer. As to outward things. If the one is sick, troubled, or distressed, the other should manifest care, tenderness, pity, and compassion, and afford all possible relief and succor. They should likewise unite their prudent counsels and endeavors, comfortably to maintain themselves and the family under their joint care. Husband and wife should be patient one toward another. If both are truly pious, yet neither of them is perfectly holy, in such cases a patient, forgiving, forbearing spirit is very needful."

Lesson 4
Answers will vary.

Lesson 5
"A voice resounds like thunder-peal,/'Mid dashing waves and clang of steel:/The Rhine, the Rhine, the German Rhine!/Who guards to-day my stream divine?/Dear Fatherland, no danger thine;/Firm stand thy sons to watch the Rhine!" And "They stand, a hundred thousand strong,/Quick to avenge their country's wrong;"

Chapter 23

Lesson 1

The country was on the verge of bankruptcy because the nation's currency was virtually worthless. When the war ended, the economy was in turmoil. Even the army was in crisis. Continental Army officers threatened military action against Congress. Armed mobs in Massachusetts closed courts and threatened a state armory.

With treaties nullified by the states, with no federal force to enforce laws, and the treasury empty, the Congress of the United States was in shambles. It called upon the states to pay their quotas of money into the treasury, only to be treated with contempt — Congress had no way to enforce its laws and the states knew it. Things were so bad that it was difficult to secure a quorum for the transaction of business!

Lesson 2

The Articles upheld state sovereignty. Article 2 stated that "each State retains its sovereignty, freedom and independence, and every power...which is not... expressly delegated to the United States...." Any amendment required unanimous consent of the states. There was a national government, of sorts, composed of a Congress, which had the power to declare war, appoint military officers, sign treaties, make alliances, appoint foreign ambassadors, and manage relations with Native Americans. It had no power to levy or to collect taxes. Congress could raise money only by asking the states for funds, borrowing from foreign governments, or selling western lands. There was no provision for national courts. And, while it could appoint military officers, it could not maintain or pay for a standing army — not without state support and funding. All states were represented equally in Congress, and nine of the 13 states had to approve a bill before it became law.

Lesson 3

The truth was that many legislators were not statesmen and really did not know how to govern their states. In every part of the country, legislative action fluctuated violently. Laws were made one year only to be repealed the next. Lands were sold by one legislature and the sales were canceled by its successor. Everyone wanted change. By the mid 1780s, many of the country's most influential leaders became convinced that state legislatures had become the greatest source of tyranny in America. In the decade after independence, the state legislatures passed more acts than in the previous century. And what laws they were! These included laws postponing repayment of debts and paper money bills, allowing debtors to repay debts with worthless paper currency.

Lesson 4

Shays' Rebellion thoroughly frightened Americans. For that and other reasons, by the spring of 1787, many national leaders believed that the nation's survival was in jeopardy. Britain's refusal to evacuate military posts, the threat of national bankruptcy, conflicts among the states, and armed rebellion in western Massachusetts accentuated the weaknesses of the Articles of Confederation. The only solution, many prominent figures were convinced, was to create an effective central government led by a strong chief executive. This led to the constitutional convention.

Lesson 5

Abigail Adams, with caution, and John Adams, with some reluctance, recognized that women still did not have rights that they deserved and needed. Case also understood that none of the advances in America dealt with the problem of slavery. There were very few, though, who saw these problems.

Chapter 24

Lesson 1

As one historian explains, "The social history of eighteenth-century America presents a fundamental paradox. In certain respects, colonial society was becoming more like English society. The power of royal governors was increasing, social distinctions were hardening, lawyers were paying closer attention to English law, and a more distinct social and political elite was gradually emerging. This was a result of the expansion of Atlantic commerce, the growth of the tobacco and rice economies, and especially the sale of land. To be sure, compared to the English aristocracy, the wealthiest merchants, planters, and landholders were much more limited in wealth and less stable in membership. Nevertheless, there was a growth of regional elites who intermarried, aped English manners, and dominated the highest levels of colonial government." At the same time, the independent-minded American colonists were going much farther. They wanted more rights, more safeguards. Americans were, as one historian explains, establishing "a tradition of republicanism" that did not exist in England.

Lesson 2

American ship owners, farmers, and fisherman profited from slavery. In fact, slavery provided most of the solvent income in the colonies. The slave plantations of the West Indies became the largest market for American agricultural products. And it was not merely a southern issue. New Englanders distilled molasses produced by slaves in the French and Dutch West Indies into rum. In summary, slaves produced the major consumer goods that were the basis of world trade during the 17th and 18th centuries. These slave-grown products stimulated a consumer revolution, enticing the masses of Britain and then Western Europe to work harder and more continuously in order to enjoy the pleasures of new consumer good. It was New World slave labor that ushered in the consumer culture that emerged at the end of the Industrial Revolution.

Lesson 3

Westerners and easterners within individual colonies also fought over issues of representation, taxation, Indian policy, and the slow establishment of governmental institutions in frontier areas. In 1764, the Paxton Boys, a group of Scotch-Irish frontier settlers from western Pennsylvania, marched on Philadelphia, and only withdrew after they were promised a greater representation in the Quaker-dominated provincial assembly and greater protection against Indians. In the late 1760s in backcountry South Carolina, where local government was largely nonexistent, frontier settlers organized themselves into vigilante groups known as Regulators to maintain order. Only extension of a new court system into the backcountry kept the Regulators from attacking Charleston. In North Carolina, in the early 1770s, the eastern militia had to suppress conflict in the backcountry, where settlers complained about underrepresentation in the colonial assembly, high taxes, exorbitant legal fees, and manipulation of debt laws by lawyers, merchants, and officials backed by eastern planters.

Lesson 4

No doubt slavery was profitable; however, it did not end when it was not. Slavery expansion, at least, ended because of the efforts of great men of God like William Wilberforce.

Lesson 5

Current U.S. immigration policy is based on the Immigration Act of 1965, which ended the national origins quota system. But, the new law still has a limit on the number of immigrants that can be admitted in a single year. This limit favors countries in the Eastern Hemisphere, in that the Western quota is 120,000, while the Eastern is 170,000. The new act also provides for the quick admittance of immigrants with needed or vital skills, such as doctors and scientists. Nonetheless, the time to be full citizens can vary from four to 23 years. From 1790 to 1795 immigration policy changed.

Chapter 25

Lesson 1

Prayer is an active affair to Guyon. She approached the Father like a proactive daughter, expecting and seeing God do miraculous things as she sat attentively at the Throne of Grace!

Lesson 2

On Being Brought to America from Africa/'Twas mercy brought me from my Pagan land,/Taught my benighted soul to understand/That there's a God, that there's a Saviour too:/Once I redemption neither fought nor knew,/Some view our sable race with scornful eye,/"Their colour is a diabolic dye."/Remember, Christians, Negroes, black as Cain,/May be refin'd, and join th' angelic train.

Lesson 3

A. Lord, Thou art Life, though I be dead;/Love's fire Thou art, however cold I be:

B. My faith burns low, my hope burns low;/Only my heart's desire cries out in me/By the deep thunder of its want and woe,/Cries out to Thee.

Lesson 4

I believe I have found the answer to these questions, and I should like to state frankly that my object in writing this book is to try to bring into some troubled Christian lives around me a little real and genuine comfort. My own idea of the religion of the Lord Jesus Christ is that it was meant to be full of comfort. I feel sure any unprejudiced reader of the New Testament would say the same; and I believe that every newly converted soul, in the first joy of its conversion, fully expects it. And yet, as I have said, it seems as if, with a large proportion of Christians, their religious lives are the most uncomfortable part of their existence. Does the fault of this state of things lie with the Lord? Has He promised more than He is able to supply?

Lesson 5

The author states, "All of God's saints — past, present, and future — are flashes of lightning in the sky. And the darkness is never the same again because the light reveals what life can be in Jesus Christ." "Memory allows possibility," theologian Walter Brueggemann writes. "A gathered inheritance. We bring memory. You bring possibility!"

Chapter 26

Lesson 1

Answers will vary. Although Jefferson believed in a Creator, his concept of it resembled that of the god of deism (the term "Nature's God" used by deists of the time). With his scientific bent, Jefferson rejected the miracles of Christianity.

Lesson 2

David Hume seems to have taken it as proved, by his time, that Christianity is not rationally defensible. His essay "On Miracles" tries to undermine a line of argument important to the Christian apologetic of the time. In his arguments Hume rejected "the greater miracle" and opted for the more "reasonable" answer. "When anyone tells me, that he saw a dead man restored to life, I immediately consider with myself, whether it be more probable, that this person should either deceive or be deceived, or that the fact, which he relates, should really have happened. I weigh the one miracle against the other; and according to the superiority, which I discover, I pronounce my decision, and always reject the greater miracle. If the falsehood of his testimony would be more miraculous, than the event which he relates; then, and not till then, can he pretend to command my belief or opinion."

Lesson 3

Paine had serious problems with Christianity. He states, "The study of theology, as it stands in the Christian churches, is the study of nothing; it is founded on nothing; it rests on no principles; it proceeds by no authority; it has no data; it can demonstrate nothing; and it admits of no conclusion."

Lesson 4

1. The Spacious Firmament on high,
   With all the blue Etherial Sky,
   And spangled Heav'ns, a Shining Frame,
   Their great Original proclaim:

2. The Moon takes up the Wondrous Tale,
   And nightly to the list'ning Earth

3. Repeats the Story of her Birth:
   Whilst all the Stars that round her burn,
   And all the Planets, in their turn,
   Confirm the Tidings as they rowl,
   And spread the Truth from Pole to Pole.

Lesson 5

Answers will vary.

Chapter 27

Lesson 1

In spite of 1848 revolutions, the 19th century saw most European nations ruled by conservative monarchs. Not that all nations were autocratic despotisms. England, for one, was one of the most democratic nations on the earth. But it is surprising that the liberal 19th century nonetheless spawned more retrogressive monarchies than republics. At the same time, the 19th century was a century of tremendous social change. The Industrial Revolution, which had begun in England during the second half of the 18th century, spread to Germany, Northern Italy, the United States, and Japan. By the end of the century, even Russia was on board. As a result, there was an emerging middle class that was challenging the status quo of a moneyed aristocracy and monarchy.

Lesson 2

Russia had no tradition of democracy. Its monarch was normally more despotic than any other European monarch. There was a legislative branch until the Duma was established and it was dissolved by Czar Nicholas. The Revolution of 1905 forced Czar Nicholas to offer concessions. He allowed the creation of a Duma, or legislative assembly. The Duma was not like the British Parliament or the American Congress. Representatives to the Duma had very limited powers and were elected under a very restricted suffrage. Government ministers were responsible to the czar, rather than to the Duma. Even so, Nicholas II actually dismissing the first two Dumas. The Duma, as an institution, survived with minimal power. As World War I approached, Russia was a nation with large, unresolved internal problems and was ripe for the Russian Revolution.

Lesson 3

In 1683, the Ottomans were at the gates of Vienna. This marked the high point of Ottoman power. By the end of the 19th century, the Ottoman Empire was mostly an empire in theory, and not in fact. Russia and Austria were its perennial enemies, with France and Britain switching alliances as their own national self-interests dictated. Hungary regained its independence from Turkey, only to be gobbled up by the Austrian empire. The Ottoman Empire's possessions on the Black Sea were threatened by the Russian empire. The Ottoman Empire, by 1900, was far more extensive in the Near East and Northern Africa. The Ottoman Turks had become the successors of the vast Islamic

Empire stretching from the Persian Gulf to Iraq, Syria, Palestine, Egypt, Libya, Tunisia, and Algeria. European powers chipped away at Ottoman possessions for the entire 19th century.

Lesson 4

The Austro-Hungarian Empire never could create a unified empire because it could not deal with ethnic discord.

Lesson 5

Napoleon, Hitler, Roosevelt—all put their mark on an era.

Chapter 28

Lesson 1

Germany upset the balance of power in Europe. The balance of both political and economic power in Europe was altered. Uneasiness in Europe led to rival alliance systems that set the stage for World War I.

Lesson 2

The prosperous city-states felt no need to be united. Competing European nations had conquered and occupied large portions of the Italian Peninsula. Finally, Italy needed a charismatic figure like Garibaldi to unite the nation.

Lesson 3

There were four principles, which were meant to 'guide' the decisions and changes that the Vienna Settlement brought about. They were: restoring the balance of power, containing France, restoring previous rulers, and rewarding and punishing those involved in the Napoleonic Wars, depending on which side they had fought on. The Congress of Vienna failed to do anything of these things, except contain France, which, in the long run, allowed Germany to get too powerful and set the stage for World War I.

Lesson 4

In April 1848, elections were held throughout France for a Constituent or National Assembly that was to write a new republican constitution. This Assembly was elected by universal manhood suffrage. Suddenly the electorate, which had been about 200,000, had risen to nine million. In December 1848, elections were held for a president of the Second Republic. Ironically, the new electorate, enfranchised by liberal, republican leadership, was far more conservative than the liberated intelligentsia. They elected the ultra conservative Louis Napoleon, the nephew of Napoleon Bonaparte. The

French had successfully formed a new government without the horrific bloodshed of 60 years before.

Lesson 5

Alfred Dreyfus (1859–1935) was a Jewish army captain who served on the French general staff. He was falsely accused of spying for Germany. In late 1894 he was tried and unjustly convicted of treason. Stripped of his rank, he was sent to Devil's Island in French Guiana for life. Shockingly, the French officer corps was willing to sacrifice an innocent man to preserve its reputation. Dreyfus was that man.

Chapter 29

Lesson 1

Civic or public life reflected competing interest groups, and although social harmony was the goal of the town's politicians, social strife was often the reality. Cincinnati was as economically volatile as it was socially diverse. All of this discord had an impact on families. Families in poverty were rising to wealth, and families of wealth were sinking to poverty. The children of common uneducated laborers, by their hard work and enterprise, were becoming nobles in intellect or wealth or office; while the children of the wealthy, weakened by indulgence, were sinking to humble status. Thus the two main family pressures in the mid-19th-century were growing individualism and economic change.

Lesson 2

With intergenerational hierarchies based on economic dependency less a factor in marriage formation, romantic love increased as a factor in courtship and in marital life. The affective aspects of family life grew increasingly important in the early decades of the nineteenth century and were extravagantly idealized by 1850. The insight, which the 21st century shares with the 19th, that autonomous "character" in children is best built through love, reinforced this emphasis in family life.

Lesson 3

Greven argued that three family types prevailed among Americans between the seventeenth century and the mid-19th century. The first of these temperaments, the "evangelical," was exhibited by groups like the Puritans, the Baptists, and the Methodists. Evangelical parents, according to Greven, were obsessed by human sinfulness and so strove for complete authority over their children and used every means to "break the will" of youngsters. In adulthood, many children reared in such families surrendered any remnant of selfhood in a cathartic conversion experience, a final submission to a demanding deity — onto whom they projected parental characteristics. The second group, dubbed "moderates" by Greven, favored a less drastic approach of molding the wills of their children by pious, moral example. Less preoccupied with human sinfulness than evangelicals, moderates sought to control rather than to annihilate the self. Finally, a third group, whom Greven calls "the genteel," indulged their children and showered them with affection.

Lesson 4

Transcendentalism spawned Unitarianism that rejected the Trinity and the divinity of Jesus Christ.

Lesson 5

In this last, tragic scene, the slave is free at last. "Give to me the precious token,/That my kindred dead may see—/Master! write it, write it quickly!/Master! write that I am free!"/At his earnest plea the master/Wrote for him the glad release."

Chapter 30

Lesson 1

President Polk said, "The cup of forbearance had been exhausted even before the recent information from the frontier of the Del Norte. But now, after reiterated menaces, Mexico has passed the boundary of the United States, has invaded our territory and shed American blood upon the American soil. She has proclaimed that hostilities have commenced, and that the two nations are now at war."

Lesson 2

Each looked for an easier triumph, and a result less fundamental and astounding. Both read the same Bible and pray to the same God, and each invokes His aid against the other. It may seem strange that any men should dare to ask a just God's assistance in wringing their bread from the sweat of other men's faces, but let us judge not, that we be not judged. The prayers of both could not be answered. That of neither has been answered fully. The Almighty has His own purposes. "Woe unto the world because of offenses; for it must needs be that offenses come, but woe to that man by whom the offense cometh." If we shall suppose that American slavery is one of those offenses which, in the providence of God, must needs come, but which, having continued through His appointed time, He now wills to remove, and that He gives to both North and South this terrible war as the woe due to those by whom

the offense came, shall we discern therein any departure from those divine attributes which the believers in a living God always ascribe to Him? Fondly do we hope, fervently do we pray, that this mighty scourge of war may speedily pass away. Yet, if God wills that it continue until all the wealth piled by the bondsman's two hundred and fifty years of unrequited toil shall be sunk, and until every drop of blood drawn with the lash shall be paid by another drawn with the sword, as was said three thousand years ago, so still it must be said "the judgments of the Lord are true and righteous altogether."

Lesson 3

Not by speeches and decisions of majorities will the greatest problems of the time be decided — that was the mistake of 1848–49 — but by iron and blood. This olive branch (he drew it from his memorandum book) I picked up in Avignon, to offer, as a symbol of peace, to the popular party: I see, however, that it is still not the time for it.

Lesson 4

This short, pithy speech, is full of emotion, pathos, and ethos (credibility). "You may take with you the satisfaction that proceeds from the consciousness of duty faithfully performed, and I earnestly pray that a merciful God will extend to you his blessing and protection. With an unceasing admiration of your constancy and devotion to your country, and a grateful remembrance of your kind and generous consideration of myself, I bid you all an affectionate farewell."

Lesson 5

Looking Glass is dead, Tu-hul-hil-sote is dead. The old men are all dead. It is the young men who now say yes or no. He who led the young men [Joseph's brother Alikut] is dead. It is cold and we have no blankets. The little children are freezing to death. My people — some of them have run away to the hills and have no blankets and no food. No one knows where they are — perhaps freezing to death. I want to have time to look for my children and see how many of them I can find. Maybe I shall find them among the dead. Hear me, my chiefs, my heart is sick and sad. From where the sun now stands I will fight no more against the white man.

Chapter 31

Lesson 1

Manjiro was reluctant initially to make contact with Americans, but, in the long run, both Japan and America prospered by the contact.

Lesson 2

Japan was closer to Hawaii than any other major nation, except the United States. Hawaii needed labor, and Japan could supply this labor.

Lesson 3

Chew says, "The Chinese laundryman does not learn his trade in China; there are no laundries in China. The women there do the washing in tubs and have no washboards or flat irons. All the Chinese laundrymen here were taught in the first place by American women just as I was taught. The reason why so many Chinese go into the laundry business in this country is because it requires little capital and is one of the few opportunities that are open. Men of other nationalities who are jealous of the Chinese, because he is a more faithful worker than one of their people, have raised such a great outcry about Chinese cheap labor that they have shut him out of working on farms or in factories or building railroads or making streets or digging sewers. He cannot practice any trade, and his opportunities to do business are limited to his own countrymen. So he opens a laundry when he quits domestic service."

Lesson 4

The Central Pacific also faced an acute labor shortage. The Civil War had required many men. In the winter of 1864, the company had only 600 laborers — far short of the 12,000 it needed. The Central Pacific turned to China to provide its labor. Within two years, 12,000 of the Central Pacific railroad's 13,500 employees were Chinese immigrants.

Lesson 5

The Chinese are persecuted, cheated, and violated. And Pun Chi continues, "Your Supreme Court has decided that the Chinese shall not bring action or give testimony against white men."

Chapter 32

Lesson 1

Most people think that nationalism is a love for one's country. Of course, it is much more. Throughout history, large groups of people who share a cultural identity (language, customs, history) have felt the pulling power of nationalistic feeling. A nation is a community of people or peoples living in a defined territory and organized under a single government. Nationalism, then, revolves around a community living in a geographical place. The nation may even be split — as Prussia was separated from Germany after World War II — but it is a nation and can exhibit nationalism. The spirit of nationalism may also think its nation is better off as an autonomous, separate state. These nations are willing to go to extreme measures in achieving autonomous self-rule. Revolutions, wars, ethnic cleansing, and other conflicts of varying degrees have occurred throughout history because of a love for one's country. Nationalism can unite people into cohesive, stable nations. Likewise, it can tear nations apart, which can result in long periods of social upheaval and political chaos.

Lesson 2

Imagination, emotion, and freedom are distinctive of romanticism. Any list of particular characteristics of the literature of romanticism includes subjectivity and an emphasis on individualism; spontaneity; freedom from rules; solitary life rather than life in society; the beliefs that imagination is superior to reason and devotion to beauty; love of and worship of nature; and fascination with the past, especially the myths and mysticism of the Middle Ages.

Lesson 3

The Gothic view encouraged emotionalism and sentimentalism. The longing for "simpler" eras not freighted with the weight of the modern world gave rise to a movement in national states, Gothic romance völkisch movement, which celebrated indigenous, folk groups, and clans within a nation's borders. The other influential characteristic of romanticism was its evocation of strong, irrational emotions — particularly horror. In a sort of reverse snobbery, romanticism, and then its first cousin, nationalism, embraced a concept called the "noble savage." Of course the motherland, or fatherland, was the center of the universe, but there were "natives" who needed to hear the "gospel" of the land. Most "natives" were depicted as inevitably lazy, unable to govern themselves. But, to the romantic, and to the nationalist, this was good. Later, this nationalism would switch to imperialism and now the nationalist desired to share their good fortune with other nations, whether they wanted it or not.

Lesson 4

For relatively moderate results nations were willing to go to war to preserve the honor and prestige of the state.

Lesson 5

All three emphasize the empathic component of nationalism. Words like "love" and "honor" and "blood" are mentioned. Nationalism becomes the ubiquitous, most important component of life. It is more important than family or even religion (God).

Chapter 33

Lesson 1

The USA Online reports: "The early United States was predominately rural. According to the 1790 census, 95 percent of the population lived in the countryside. The 5 percent of Americans living in urban areas (places with more than 2,500 persons) lived mostly in small villages. Only Philadelphia, New York, and Boston had more than 15,000 inhabitants. The South was almost completely rural. After 1830 the urban areas of the country grew more rapidly than the rural areas. By 1890 industrialization had produced substantial growth in cities, and 35 percent of Americans lived in urban areas, mostly in the northern half of the United States. The South remained rural, except for New Orleans and a few smaller cities. The number of Americans living in cities did not surpass the number in rural areas until 1920. . . . The Industrial Revolution of the 19th and 20th centuries transformed urban life and gave people higher expectations for improving their standard of living. The increased number of jobs, along with technological innovations in transportation and housing construction, encouraged migration to cities. Development of railroads, streetcars, and trolleys in the 19th century enabled city boundaries to expand. People no longer had to live within walking distance of their jobs. With more choices about where to live, people tended to seek out neighbors of similar social status, if they could afford to do so. The wealthy no longer had to live in the center of the city, so they formed exclusive enclaves far from warehouses, factories, and docks. Office buildings, retail shops, and light manufacturing characterized the central business districts. Heavier industry clustered along the rivers and rail lines that brought in raw materials and shipped out finished products. Railroads also allowed goods to be brought into downtown commercial districts. . . . The growth of cities outpaced the ability of local governments to extend clean water, garbage collection, and sewage systems into poorer areas, so conditions in cities deteriorated. Cities in the late 19th century were large, crowded, and impersonal places devoted to making money. Not surprisingly, corruption was rampant in city government and city services, in the construction industry, and among landlords and employers. High rents, low wages, and poor services produced misery in the midst of unprecedented economic growth." In summary, industrial expansion and population growth significantly changed the face of the nation's cities. Noise, slums, air pollution, and sanitation became commonplace. The infrastructure of the 19th century city could not sustain rapid urban growth, however, and this caused many problems.

http://www.theusaonline.com/people/urbanization.htm

Lesson 2

The cost of building up, instead of out, was much cheaper. A 14-story building more than doubled the profits of a seven story building, and the cost to build on top of existing structures was much cheaper than building onto existing structures.

Lesson 3

Once Americans grew comfortable with political parties and political opposition, they began to embrace a sort of governing strategy that was narcissistic. This was especially true in the city where large groups of voters could be motivated and manipulated. Thus, political corruption was rampant. In a country where there was no FBI or other federal police agency, there was no external enforcement agency in a city or town. May Americans, too, were delighted to find a way to get rich quick.

Lesson 4

The fire probably started in Mrs. O'Leary's barn. The fire raged out of control for a day and a half. The fire destroyed four-and-a-half square miles of Chicago — some 17,500 buildings. All of downtown was destroyed. At times, temperatures reached 1,500 to 1,800 degrees. People were literally incinerated; limestone disintegrated into powder. 250 people died, 200 were listed as missing, and 100,000 people were homeless.

Lesson 5

Magnuson points out that revivalist movements like the Salvation Army, the Volunteers of America, the Christian and Missionary Alliance, and the "Rescue Movement" attempted some of the most ambitious and innovative urban redevelopment projects that America knew in the Gilded Age. Revivalist social reformers were able to reinforce the already natural link between revivalism and social reform. The revivalists saw soul-salvation as the only hope for society, to be sure. But obedience to biblical injunctions to preach the Gospel to all people, in the evangelical revivalist mind, also required a profound empathic identity with the poor. This movement was, and Magnuson does not point this out, an aberration in the American religious scene. Remember that the famous Philadelphia Baptist preacher Russell Conwell was preaching his famous sermon "Acres of Diamonds" to millions of people. Religious giants like Andrew Carnegie expressed the ethic most clearly in an article entitled, "The Gospel of Wealth" (1889). In general, mainline Christianity praised wealth and unabashedly used it as a yardstick for spirituality. Riches was a sure sign of godliness, and the power of money to do good was stressed. This attitude is in direct contrast to men like D. L. Moody who never made a general appeal for money. And, while the Revivalists did not extol poverty, they saw the poor as victims of systemic evil more than congenital, lazy people. Moody, Gladden, and others became some of the best late 19th-century American social engineers. They understood firsthand the structural and environmental causes of poverty and social oppression. They offered, for their day, quite sophisticated and enlightened social welfare interventions. Fresh air programs, homes for women, farm colonies — these were really very elaborate and in some cases expensive and in some cases very successful. While some of their programs were temporary, hand-out charity, some programs sincerely sought for more long-term solutions. And while some programs sought to move folks out of the city to rural environments, and did betray a somewhat anti-urban bias, other solutions offered amazing answers that celebrated the city and sought to rehabilitate it — not abandon the city.

Chapter 34

Lesson 1

Most items are more expensive. Some of the vegetables, and one meat choice, cost about the same. One would find far more packaged goods, and, of course, there were no fast food options. However, at the same time, among high-end restaurants, food is still prepared from scratch. Finally, there are many, many more choices of food in local supermarkets.

Lesson 2

I walked downtown to attend to some business and had to take an elevator in an office building. I stood waiting for the elevator, and when the others, all of whom were white, got in, I made a move to go in also, and the boy shut the cage door in my face. I thought the elevator was too crowded and waited; the same thing happened the second time. I would have walked up, but I was going to the fifth story, and my long walk downtown had tired me. The third time the elevator came down, the boy pointed to a sign and said, "I guess you can't read; but n*****s don't ride in this elevator, we're white folks here, we are. . . ." The very first humiliation I received I remember very distinctly to this day. It was when I was very young. A little girl playmate said to me: "I like to come over to your house to play, we have such good times, and your ma has such good preserves; but don't you tell my ma I eat over here. My ma says you

all are nice, clean folks and she'd rather live by you than the white people we moved away from; for you don't borrow things. I know she would whip me if I ate with you, tho, because you are colored, you know."

Lesson 3

I did not strike because I wanted to; I struck because I had to. A miner the same as any other workman must earn fair living wages, or he can't live. And it is not how much you get that counts. It is how much what you get will buy. I have gone through it all, and I think my case is a good sample.

Lesson 4

She wanted to be a stay-at-home mom, but could not because she was a widow! I think that she also enjoyed the fellowship that working out of the home offered her. She had a good job! "You see, I have really done my best to fulfill what the ministers and others often tell us is the true destiny of a woman to be a wife and mother. But the fates have been against me. My second husband had incipient consumption when I married him, altho neither of us knew it. He died after a short illness and six months later my little boy was born Before the baby was a month old I was back in the factory, a starcher girl once more. Except for this interval of six years I have earned my living starching collars at four cents the dozen. I have managed to bring up my two children fairly well. They have gone to school and my daughter has had music and dancing lessons."

Lesson 5

It is while I am getting dinner that Ruth and Mary have their book lessons. We do not care to have our children enter school before the third grade because of the class of children that attend our ward school. The two little girls use a wooden box for a desk, sitting on two lower ones, in a snug corner of the kitchen, where I can teach them as I peel potatoes, pare apples or move about the room mixing a pudding. It takes some time to prepare a meal for seven people, four of them hungry students. One thing that makes it harder is not having any water or sink in the house. By half after twelve the dinner is on the table, and I have spent a morning in careful planning, with quick, sure strokes to get all the work done, and yet have time to stop occasionally, as I have to, to teach the children. They come first, after all.

☞ Exam Answer Keys

Chapter 1 Exam Options

Option 1 – Matching:
1. L'Anse aux Meadows: The Newfoundland Viking settlement.
2. Caravel: Fast, technological advanced ships that expanded exploration overseas.
3. Mariner's Compass: A more advanced compass used to navigate ships.
4. Lead Line: Used to measure the depth of water.
5. Astrolabe: A navigation tool to calculate longitude and latitude of ships.

Option 2 – Essay:
Answers will vary.

Chapter 2 Exam Options

Option 1 – Matching:
1. Homogeneous population: A group of people with similar traits.
2. Eastern Woodlands: A forested area stretching from the Atlantic coast west to the Great Lakes and southward from Maine to North Carolina.
3. Warrior chiefs: Leaders chosen for their bravery, acumen, and style.
4. The Iroquois League: Combined a central authority with tribal autonomy and provided a model for the federal system of government later adopted by the United States.
5. Ethnocentrism: Making value judgments about another culture from the perspective of one's own culture.

Option 2 – Essay:
Answers will vary. The most effective evangelists among the Native Peoples were always European evangelists who lived among the Native Americans and adopted some of their cultural choices (e.g., food and clothing).

Chapter 3 Exam Options

Option 1 – Matching:
1. Cartography: The science of mapmaking.
2. Northwest Passage: An alleged shortcut from Europe to the Orient by going west.
3. Age of Exploration: An era of vigorous exploration of the New World.

4. Primary source: A document that is firsthand information, found to be more reliable.
5. Secondary source: A document that is based on secondhand information and not considered as reliable

Option 2 – Essay:
First, Shaw is obviously an anglophile who really likes Sir Francis Drake. The story he recounts is more or less a biased view of this controversial man. One would expect, for instance, a Spanish historian to have an entirely different version of the same story. Shaw's "history" is really historical fiction, based on some fact. It is similar to books written by G. A. Henty.

Chapter 4 Exam Options

Option 1 – Matching:
1. Stereotype: Oversimplified types.
2. Accommodation: To participate or to cooperate with competing forces.
3. Nation building: Act of building a nation usually in the spirit and image of the creating institution.
4. Jamestown: The first permanent English settlement.
5. William Penn: Founder of the Quakers.

Option 2 – Essay:
In the 18th century, waves of western settlers pounded against the borders of Indian lands. Yet the course of events that led to Native American survival were not inevitable. America's first president, George Washington, and his Secretary of War Henry Knox claimed to respect Indian rights and promised to secure Indian lands for white settlement only through treaty and purchase. However, at most every turn, Native Americans found themselves overwhelmed by Anglo-Americans' military resources. But their response to events was neither one-dimensional nor defeatist. Some tried diplomacy. Others turned to religion. Still others tried to deflate white antagonism by embracing the economic and cultural values of their enemies. Some worked the legal system skillfully. Others found success in war. Some even turned philanthropists' well-intentioned but ethnocentric plans for their assimilation into a basis for political organization. Ultimately all attempts failed (Internet).

Chapter 5 Exam Options

Option 1 – Matching:
1. Duman: Russian legislative branch.

2. Nationalist revolts: Revolutions stimulated by nationalist agendas.

3. Technological innovation: technological, scientific advances related to new products.

4. Capital accumulation: The collection of wealth for investment.

5. Total war: A war that affects soldiers and civilians.

Option 2 – Essay:

Inevitably healthy, diverse economies generate urban centers that are completely dependent upon thriving agrarian centers to feed them. That was as completely true with the earliest cities in Mesopotamia to Paris in 1750. If there was not abundant food available, then there could not be healthy economies.

Chapter 6 Exam Options

Option 1 – Matching:

1. Humanists: Scholars who focused on classic works and human achievement.

2. Grievance mentality: A mindset that reacts against a certain notion or philosophy.

3. Johannes Gutenberg: Used movable type to print papal documents and the first printed version of the Bible.

4. Renaissance: Literally means "rebirth."

5. Desiderius Erasmus: A Dutch humanist.

Option 2 – Essay:

Answers will vary.

Chapter 7 Exam Options

Option 1 – Matching:

1. Beaux-Art: Art whose sole purpose is to bring beauty vs. art to glorify God.

2. Aesthetic: Art appreciation.

3. Parthenon: Greek Athenian temple.

4. Baroque: a "modern" artistic style that emphasized light and shadow.

5. Chiaroscuro: Gold highlighting in Renaissance painting.

Option 2 – Essay:

Beauty is beauty, and certainly God creates all things. The problem with beaux-arts is that it opens a Pandora's Box. If we produce art that brings pleasure without any notion of glorifying God, how far will that go? Where this took us, in the 21st century, is to a disturbing, no limit, self-serving "weird" art that brings glory to no

one, least of all God, and at times appears to be ugly, not beautiful.

Chapter 8 Exam Options

Option 1 – Matching:

1. Martin Luther: Started the Protestant Reformation.

2. Pope Leo X: The pope who confronted Luther.

3. John Calvin: Swiss reformer who championed the Reformed position.

4. John Knox: A Scottish reformer.

5. Anabaptists: Early dissenters who preferred believer baptism and pacifism.

Option 2 – Essay:

Answers will vary.

Chapter 9 Exam Options

Option 1 – Matching:

1. Constitutional governments: Government by consent of the governed through written documents.

2. Peace of Westphalia: The treaty that ended the Thirty Years' War.

3. Moral absolutism: Society controlled completely by one person or small group.

4. Authority: The essential characteristic of all government, whatever its form.

5. Absolutism: Government that makes all the choices for everyone.

Option 2 – Essay:

Answers will vary. Government is part of the order of creation and a minister of God (Rom. 13:4). Christians are to obey governmental authorities (Rom. 13:1–4, 1 Peter 2:13–14). Christians are also to be the salt of the earth and the light of the world (Matt. 5:13–16) in the midst of the political context.

Chapter 10 Exam Options

Option 1 – Matching:

1. Epistemology: The study of knowledge.

2. The deductive approach: Starts with commonsense observations and moves toward complex conclusions.

3. The inductive approach: Starts with objective facts.

4. Copernicus: A scientist who argued that the sun, not the earth, was the center of the universe.

5. Imperialism: The policy of extending the rule or influence of a country over other countries or colonies.

Option 2 – Essay:

The Roman Catholic Church regrets some of the excesses of the Galileo trial, but Galileo was without a doubt, belligerent and disrespectful in his views. Also, he was wrong — he argued that the planets circled the sun in perfect circles. The biggest problem with Galileo was that he mixed theology and science — it wasn't so much that the Church mixed theology with science. "In 1616, the year of Galileo's first "trial," there was precious little elasticity in Catholic biblical theology. The Church had just been through the bruising battles of the Reformation. One of the chief quarrels with the Protestants was over the private interpretation of Scripture. Catholic theologians were in no mood to entertain hermeneutical injunctions from a layman like Galileo. His friend Archbishop Piero Dini warned him that he could write freely so long as he 'kept out of the sacristy.' But Galileo threw caution to the winds, and it was on this point — his apparent trespassing on the theologians' turf — that his enemies were finally able to nail him." http://www.catholiceducation.org/articles/history/world/wh0005.html

Chapter 11 Exam Options

Option 1 – Matching:
1. Manumission: To free from slavery.
2. Sub-Saharan Africa: Below the Sahara Desert.
3. Islamic Traders: Islamic commercial traders, mostly in slaves.
4. Atlantic slave trade: A slave business administered by Europeans between the West Indies and Africa.
5. Slave trades: Contributed to the development of powerful African states.

Option 2 – Essay:
Slavery was so profitable, many white traders intentionally looked the other way or even ignored the moral implications of their acts altogether.

Chapter 12 Exam Options

Option 1 – Matching:
1. Plantations: Agricultural businesses that raised valuable crops.
2. Indentured servants: Servants who were obligated to work for a few years but then were freed.

3. Maroon colonies: Colonies full of racially mixed people.
4. Race mixing: Marriage across racial lines.
5. Chattel slavery: Slaves are considered as "chattel" or personal property.

Option 2 – Essay:
Answers will vary.

Chapter 13 Exam Options

Option 1 – Matching:
1. Papacy: The pope and his office.
2. Cola di Rienzi: An Italian nobleman who really wanted the papacy returned to Rome.
3. House of Hanover: Replaced the Stuarts in the monarchy of England.
4. Popular sovereignty: Government instituted for the right of people, not the government.
5. Natural rights: Rights given by God, not by man.

Option 2 – Essay:
The American Revolution was successful. The French Revolution simply replaced one monarch with another one. Answers will vary.

Chapter 14 Exam Options

Option 1 – Matching:
1. Count Nikolaus Ludwig von Zinzendorf: A Moravian nobleman who started the Herrnhut communities.
2. Moravian Church: A pietistic, 1700 church.
3. Herrnhut : Moravian communities famous for missionary work and a 100-year prayer meeting.
4. Anabaptists: Radicals who embraced pacifism and believer baptism.
5. Manifest Destiny: The view that Americans were destined to rule the North American continent.

Option 2 – Essay:
While Franklin did not agree with Whitefield's theological views, he admired his "benevolent" works.

Chapter 15 Exam Options

Option 1 – Matching:
1. Septuagint: The Old Testament in Greek.
2. Latin Vulgate Bible: An early Roman Catholic Bible.
3. Geneva Bible: An early Protestant translation.

4. King James Bible: The official British government translation in the early 17th century.

5. Athanasius: Christian theologian, bishop of Alexandria, Church Father, and noted Egyptian leader.

Option 2 – Essay:

Answer will vary. There are many choices: Dietrich Bonhoeffer was a loyal German who reluctantly opposed the leadership of his country.

Chapter 16 Exam Options

Option 1 – Matching:

1. Covenant: A contract between two consenting parties.

2. Hartford Convention: A 19th-century declaration of independence, of sorts, by New England.

3. Wampanoags: Native people in New England.

4. Massachusetts Declaration of Rights of 1661: A statement of English rights.

5. Sir Edmund Andros: Controversial English governor in New England.

Option 2 – Essay:

Until recently, America was a predominantly Christian nation that celebrated Christian morality and values. The importance of local governments, the sense of covenant that exists between public officials and constituents remains, and generally speaking the notion of hard work is valued.

Chapter 17 Exam Options

Option 1 – Matching:

1. Seven Years' War: The French and Indian War between France and England (primarily).

2. Redemptioners: A kind of indentured servant.

3. History: A collection of individual narratives.

4. Mary Cooper: Began her diary at age 54 while tending the family farmstead with her husband.

5. Gottlieb Mittelberger: A schoolteacher who left his wife and children to travel to America.

Option 2 – Essay:
Answers will vary.

Chapter 18 Exam Options

Option 1 – Matching:

1. Boston Massacre: A 1770 incident where British soldiers fired on American citizens.

2. Sons of Liberty: A secret organization of American patriots.

3. Declaration of Independence: A declaration of American rights written in 1776.

4. Constitutional Convention: A meeting to write a new constitution.

5. Continental Congress in 1782: The ruling national legislature at the end of the American Revolution.

Option 2 – Essay:

This is unfortunately not an uncommon combination — Samson was a great leader but notoriously immoral believer. Likewise Solomon may have been very wise, but he made some very unwise decisions in his relationships with foreign wives. It is a mystery how God uses everyone — including the author, who, like all believers, is saved by grace through faith.

Chapter 19 Exam Options

Option 1 – Matching:

1. Mayflower: The ship that brought the Pilgrims to Plymouth.

2. Courtship: Social relation to prepare for marriage.

3. Vacation: An interlude, rest away from work.

4. Midwives: Older women who relied on practical experience in delivering children.

5. East: Original headstones faced this direction awaiting the Day of Resurrection.

Option 2 – Essay:

Most 18th-century Americans experienced the death of one or both of their parents by the time they were married. As a result, a majority of colonial Americans probably spent some time in a step family. Likewise, today, the majority of Americans spend their childhoods in blended families —but not because of death but because of divorce. Many 17th-century young people started working when they were 14–15; today, American youth work in their late teens. Perhaps the biggest difference between families then and now is that colonial society placed relatively little emphasis on familial privacy. Community authorities and neighbors supervised and intervened in family life. In New England, selectmen oversaw ten or twelve families, removed children from "unfit" parents, and ensured that fathers exercised proper family government. Finally, a major difference between 17th-century families and today is in the role of the father. The historian Stephen Mintz explains, "In theory, the seventeenth-century family was a hierarchical unit, in which the father was invested with patriarchal authority. He alone sat in an armed chair, his symbolic throne, while other household members sat on benches or stools. He taught children to write, led household prayers, and carried on the bulk of correspondence with family members. Domestic conduct manuals were addressed to him, not to his wife. Legally, the father was the primary parent. Fathers, not mothers, received custody of children after divorce or separation. In colonial New England, a father was authorized to correct and punish insubordinate wives, disruptive children, and unruly servants. He was also responsible for placing his children in a lawful calling and for consenting to his children's marriages. His control over inheritance kept his grown sons dependent upon him for years, while they waited for the landed property they needed to establish an independent household. A revolution has taken place in family life since the late 1960s. Today, two-thirds of all married women with children —and an even higher proportion of single mothers — work outside the home, compared to just 16 percent in 1950. Half of all marriages end in divorce — twice the rate in 1966 and three times the rate in 1950. Three children in ten are born out of wedlock. Over a quarter of all children now live with only one parent and fewer than half of live with both their biological mother and father. Meanwhile, the proportion of women who remain unmarried and childless has reached a record high; fully twenty percent of women between the ages of 30 and 34 have not married and over a quarter have had no children, compared to six and eight percent, respectively, in 1970."

Chapter 20 Exam Options

Option 1 – Matching:

1. Battle of Narva: That battle that showed Sweden was a major power.
2. Battle of Blenheim: The battle that ended French domination of the continent until Napoleon.
3. Battle of Quebec: The battle that assured English domination of North America.
4. Battle of Lexington and Concord: The battle that precipitated the American Revolution.
5. Battle of Hohenlinden: Napoleon's France was the premier power of Europe again.

Option 2 – Essay:

Gunpowder came onto the world stage in the form of muskets and artillery, giving rise to Dragoon units, the infantrymen, and grenadiers. This was the age of Montcalm, Wolfe, and Bonaparte. Rifles replaced muskets. Adversaries could kill opponents at 100 yards. Causalties actually declined, but 18th-century warfare presaged a new, ominous military challenge.

Chapter 21 Exam Options

Option 1 – Matching:

1. Enlightenment: A period of great progress in science and knowledge in general.
2. Theory of Evolution: A theory about the origin of species.
3. Karl Linnaeus: Invented a classification for living things.
4. Jacques Turgot: French social thinker and economist.
5. Dissenters: The Dissenters were a sort of Unitarian Universalist church.

Option 2 – Essay:

We are able to control the Internet and yet we have no creative solutions to age-old problems like unemployment. Answers will vary.

Chapter 22 Exam Options

Option 1 – Matching:

1. Olaudah Equiano: A former slave who wrote narrative stories about his slave experience.
2. Marquis de la Galissonière: French nobleman who wrote about New France.
3. The Boston Latin Grammar School: One of the first public schools.
4. Max Schneckenburger: German poet.
5. Jean le Rond d'Alembert: French philosopher.

Option 2 – Essay:

And all thing considered, it would conduce more to the Welfare of the Province, to have White Servants for a Term of Years, than to have Slaves for Life . . . It is likewise most lamentable to think, how in taking Negros out of Africa, and selling of them here, That which GOD has joined together men to boldly rend asunder; Men from their Country, Husbands from their Wives, Parents from their Children. How horrible is the Uncleanness, Mortality, if not Murder, that the Ships are guilty of that bring great Crouds of these miserable Men, and Women.

Chapter 23 Exam Options

Option 1 – Matching:

1. Articles of Confederation: American government until 1789.
2. Shays' Rebellion: A rebellion caused by dysfunctional nature of the Articles of Confederation.
3. Democratic republic: Form of government elected by the people to represent them.
4. State sovereignty: States have governing authority over that of a central government.
5. The Declaration of Independence: Document that established a foundation for U.S. governance.

Option 2 – Essay:

There are several examples. For example, Pearl Harbor was a catastrophe that ultimately saved England. It is doubtful England could have won World War II without America.

Chapter 24 Exam Options

Option 1 – Matching:

1. Peter Zenger: First major freedom of the press trial in America.
2. John Woolman: Early American abolitionist.
3. Toussaint Louverture: Leader of Haitian Revolution.
4. Quaker opposition: These Christians founded the first American antislavery group.
5. Eric Williams: Wrote the book *Capitalism and Slavery*.

Option 2 – Essay:

With growing problems in government, and the collapse of time-honored institutions (e.g., education), Americans are justifiably skeptical. Yet, Christians, at least, have every reason to be optimistic! Greater is He that is in us than he that is in the world! We know that our God is in total control of all things!

Chapter 25 Exam Options

Option 1 – Matching:

1. Madame Guyon: A great woman of intercessory prayer.
2. Phillis Wheatley: A slave poet of great ability.
3. Christina Rossetti: A British writer and saint.
4. Hanna Smith: A great woman of holiness and faith.
5. Quietism: An assertive sort of passive resistance.

Option 2 – Essay:

Gals 3:28 does not abolish all earthly relationships. Rather, it puts these relationships in the perspective of salvation history. As Paul goes on to say, "And if you are Christ's then you are Abraham's offspring, heirs according to promise" (Gal. 3:29; cf. also Rom. 10:2). All who are in Christ have the same status before God; but they do not necessarily have the same function (1976, 570). Galatians 3:28 is certainly in harmony with 1 Peter 3:7, which makes it clear that women are "joint-heirs of the grace of life. (Colin Brown).

Chapter 26 Exam Options

Option 1 – Matching:

1. The Jefferson Bible: An interpretation of Scripture that removed references to the miracles and divinity of Christ.
2. David Hume: A philosopher who questioned the existence of miracles.
3. Thomas Paine: An opportunistic atheist and capable writer.
4. John Wesley: Father of the United Methodist Church.
5. William Wilberforce: British statesman who ended slavery expansion in England.

Option 2 – Essay:

Answers will vary.

Chapter 27 Exam Options

Option 1 – Matching:

1. Revolutions in 1848: European nationalist revolutions in 1848.
2. Industrial Revolution: Movement that began in England but spread to the whole world.
3. Colonization: European policy of expansion.
4. Middle Class Entrepreneur: Important socio-economic class that grew powerful in the 18th century.
5. Laborer: A new class of people who were employed in factories.
6. Crimean War of 1853–56: War between Russia and England and her western allies.
7. Czar Alexander II: 19th-century Russian Emperor.
8. Russo-Japanese War of 1904–05: A complete victory of the Japanese over the Russians.

9. Duma : Russian parliament.
10. Franz Joseph: Habsburg dynasty monarch who ruled the Austro-Hungarian Empire for over 50 years.

Option 2 – Essay:

One was the fulfillment of the revolutionary promise to give all Europe political liberty — the vote for all men, a free press, a parliament, and a written constitution. Between 1815 and 1888 many outbreaks occurred for this cause.

Chapter 28 Exam Options

Option 1 – Matching:

1. Otto von Bismarck: Great nationalist leader of Greater Germany.
2. Giuseppe Garibaldi: Italian patriot who unified Italy into a nation/state.
3. Congress Of Vienna: Ended the Napoleonic wars.
4. Archduke Maximilian: Austrian who ruled Mexico with French support.
5. Alfred Dreyfus: Jewish French officer unjustly charged for treason.

Option 2 – Essay:

Tragically, things were about the same, except now it was Germany, not France, who was on center stage.

Chapter 29 Exam Options

Option 1 – Matching:

1. Abolitionists: Antislavery activists.
2. Transcendentalism: 19th-century movement that celebrated the subjective and nature.
3. Corporal punishment: Physical penalty or pain used to deter or discipline a child.
4. Unitarian Church: Founded by the transcendentalists.
5. Ralph Waldo Emerson: A leading proponent of transcendentalism.

Option 2 – Essay:

This author agrees with Miller and other intellectual historians (e.g., Handlin, Bailyn, Leach). The truth is evangelical marriages manifested fewer family problems than other marriages. Birth rates were greater. Life expectancy longer. One has only to read the poetry of Anne Bradstreet to know the depth of affection manifested in 18th-century evangelical marriages.

Chapter 30 Exam Options

Option 1 – Matching:

1. James K. Polk: President of the United States who declared war on Germany.
2. Abraham Lincoln: President of the United States during the American Civil War.
3. Otto von Bismarck: Prime Minister during German unification.
4. Robert E. Lee: Confederate commander.
5. Chief Joseph: Native American chief.

Option 2 – Essay:

Historian Richard Hofstadter argues that Americans require a mediocre, middle of the road, no idealism president. He argues that no one as ugly but principled a man as Abraham would be elected president!

Chapter 31 Exam Options

Option 1 – Matching:

1. Nakahama Manjiro: Japanese American who facilitated understanding between both countries.
2. William Hooper: American sugar cane industrialist in Hawaii who employed many Japanese workers.
3. Lee Chew: Asian-American immigrant.
4. Chinese Exclusion Act: Anti-Chinese immigration law at the end of the 19th century.
5. Pun Chi: Chinese statesmen who wrote a critical letter to the U. S. Congress.

Option 2 – Essay:

There were some racial reasons. The California Supreme Court rules that a Chinese witness could not testify against a white man accused of murder. After George Hall was convicted of the murder of Ling Sing, based on the testimony of three Chinese witnesses, Hall's lawyer argued that a California statute barring testimony by African-Americans, mulattoes, and Indians applied to all non-whites. There was a fear that the Chinese would overwhelm white, American communities. The court concurred. The Exclusion Act began, "Whereas, in the opinion of the Government of the United States the coming of Chinese laborers to this country endangers the good order of certain localities within the territory thereof."

Chapter 32 Exam Options

Option 1 – Matching:

1. Nationalism: A movement that celebrates the peculiarities and specialness of a geographical area.

2. Imperialism: A movement where a country seeks to colonize or control or both other areas of the world.

3. Nation Building: When a nation seeks to "help" another country build its economy, government, and society.

4. Romanticism: A world view that celebrates the subjective and individualism. Gothic Romance: A romantic, dark, sometimes horrible theme that emerges at the end of the 19th century.

5. Völkisch Movement: A folk, indigenous national movement.

Option 2 – Essay:
Answers will vary.

Chapter 33 Exam Options

Option 1 – Matching:

1. Industrial Expansion: After the American Civil War, a significant industrial expansion.

2. Tenement housing: Urban housing where individuals lived in adjoining apartments.

3. Boss Tweed: A dishonest, powerful 19th-century New York City politician.

4. Great Chicago Fire: Fire that destroyed most of Chicago.

5. D. L. Moody: Evangelist with an outreach in Chicago.

Option 2 – Essay:
The notion of controlled urban growth occurred to no one. But it would have been a good idea. While social welfare was unknown, encouraging, even enriching, evangelical outreaches would have also ameliorated urban areas.

Chapter 34 Exam Options

Option 1 – Matching:

1. American Missionary Association: A Protestant-based abolitionist group founded on September 3, 1846, in Albany, New York.

2. Miner's asthma: A euphemism for black lung disease.

3. Collar starcher: One who worked with laundry for a living.

4. Iron molder: One skilled in metalworking.

5. Homeschool: An educational methodology where parents have the role of educator.

Option 2 – Essay:
Answers will vary.

Equipping students to
Live, Write, & Speak
Communication Courses from a Biblical Worldview

- Each 34 week course develops written & verbal communication skills
- Chapters include one daily lesson Monday through Thursday with concept builders, weekly writing assignment/speech, and chapter exam on Friday.
- Learning activities include writing, essays, research paper, & public speaking

Skills for Rhetoric helps Jr. high students develop the skills necessary to communicate powerfully through writing and to articulate their thoughts clearly. Dr. Stobaugh weaves biblical concepts, readings, and applications throughout the curriculum to help equip students to stand firm in their faith.

nlpg.com/rhetoric

Skills for Literary Analysis equips Jr. high students to analyze classic literary genres, discern authors' worldviews, and apply biblical standards. Dr. Stobaugh's instruction helps to empower students to be more effective Christian apologists.

nlpg.com/literaryanalysis

Skills for Rhetoric (student)
Paper (300 pages)
Price: $34.99
ISBN: 978-0-89051-710-9

Teacher:
Paper (294 pages)
Price: $15.99
ISBN: 978-0-89051-711-6

Skills for Literary Analysis (student)
Paper (382 pages)
Price: $34.99
ISBN: 978-0-89051-712-3

Teacher:
Paper (294 pages)
Price: $15.99
ISBN: 978-0-89051-713-0

Master Books®
A Division of New Leaf Publishing Group
www.masterbooks.net

Place your order at masterbooks.net or call 800-999-3777

Now turn your favorite **Master Books** into curriculum! Each Parent Lesson Plan (PLP) includes:

- An easy-to-follow, one-year educational calendar
- Helpful worksheets, quizzes, tests, and answer keys
- Additional teaching helps and insights
- Complete with all you need to quickly and easily begin your education program today!

ELEMENTARY ZOOLOGY

1 year
4th – 6th

Package Includes: *World of Animals, Dinosaur Activity Book, The Complete Aquarium Adventure, The Complete Zoo Adventure, Parent Lesson Planner*

5 Book Package
978-0-89051-747-5 $84.99

SCIENCE STARTERS: ELEMENTARY PHYSICAL & EARTH SCIENCE

1 year
3rd – 8th grade

6 Book Package Includes: *Forces & Motion – Student, Student Journal, and Teacher; The Earth – Student, Teacher & Student Journal; Parent Lesson Planner*

6 Book Package
978-0-89051-748-2 $51.99

SCIENCE STARTERS: ELEMENTARY CHEMISTRY & PHYSICS

1 year
3rd – 8th grade

Package Includes: *Matter – Student, Student Journal, and Teacher; Energy – Student, Teacher, & Student Journal; Parent Lesson Planner*

7 Book Package
978-0-89051-749-9 $54.99

INTRO TO METEOROLOGY & ASTRONOMY

1 year
7th – 9th grade
½ Credit

Package Includes: *The Weather Book; The Astronomy Book; Parent Lesson Planner*

3 Book Package
978-0-89051-753-6 $44.99

INTRO TO OCEANOGRAPHY & ECOLOGY

1 year
7th – 9th grade
½ Credit

Package Includes: *The Ocean Book; The Ecology Book; Parent Lesson Planner*

3 Book Package
978-0-89051-754-3 $45.99

INTRO TO SPELEOLOGY & PALEONTOLOGY

1 year
7th – 9th grade
½ Credit

Package Includes: *The Cave Book; The Fossil Book; Parent Lesson Planner*

3 Book Package
978-0-89051-752-9 $44.99

CONCEPTS OF MEDICINE & BIOLOGY

1 year
7th – 9th grade
½ Credit

Package Includes: *Exploring the History of Medicine; Exploring the World of Biology; Parent Lesson Planner*

3 Book Package
978-0-89051-756-7 $40.99

CONCEPTS OF MATHEMATICS & PHYSICS

1 year
7th – 9th grade
½ Credit

Package Includes: *Exploring the World of Mathematics; Exploring the World of Physics; Parent Lesson Planner*

3 Book Package
978-0-89051-757-4 $40.99

CONCEPTS OF EARTH SCIENCE & CHEMISTRY

1 year
7th – 9th grade

Package Includes: *Exploring Planet Earth; Exploring the World of Chemistry; Parent Lesson Planner*

3 Book Package
978-0-89051-755-0 $40.99

THE SCIENCE OF LIFE: BIOLOGY

1 year
8th – 9th grade
½ Credit

Package Includes: *Building Blocks in Science; Building Blocks in Life Science; Parent Lesson Planner*

3 Book Package
978-0-89051-758-1 $44.99

BASIC PRE-MED

1 year
8th – 9th grade
½ Credit

Package Includes: *The Genesis of Germs; The Building Blocks in Life Science; Parent Lesson Planner*

3 Book Package
978-0-89051-759-8 $43.99

INTRO TO ASTRONOMY

1 year
7th – 9th grade
½ Credit

Package Includes: *The Stargazer's Guide to the Night Sky; Parent Lesson Planner*

2 Book Package
978-0-89051-760-4 $47.99

INTRO TO ARCHAEOLOGY & GEOLOGY

1 year
7th – 9th
½ Credit

Package Includes: *The Archaeology Book; The Geology Book; Parent Lesson Planner*

3 Book Package
978-0-89051-751-2 $45.99

SURVEY OF SCIENCE HISTORY & CONCEPTS

1 year
10th – 12th grade
1 Credit

Package Includes: *The World of Mathematics; The World of Physics; The World of Biology; The World of Chemistry; Parent Lesson Planner*

5 Book Package
978-0-89051-764-2 $72.99

SURVEY OF SCIENCE SPECIALTIES

1 year
10th – 12th grade
1 Credit

Package Includes: *The Cave Book; The Fossil Book; The Geology Book; The Archaeology Book; Parent Lesson Planner*

5 Book Package
978-0-89051-765-9 $81.99

SURVEY OF ASTRONOMY

1 year
10th – 12th grade
1 Credit

Package Includes: *The Stargazers Guide to the Night Sky; Our Created Moon; Taking Back Astronomy; Our Created Moon DVD; Created Cosmos DVD; Parent Lesson Planner*

4 Book, 2 DVD Package
978-0-89051-766-6 $113.99

GEOLOGY & BIBLICAL HISTORY

1 year
8th – 9th
1 Credit

Package Includes: *Explore the Grand Canyon; Explore Yellowstone; Explore Yosemite & Zion National Parks; Your Guide to the Grand Canyon; Your Guide to Yellowstone; Your Guide to Zion & Bryce Canyon National Parks; Parent Lesson Planner.*

4 Book, 3 DVD Package
978-0-89051-750-5 $108.99

PALEONTOLOGY: LIVING FOSSILS

1 year
10th – 12th grade
½ Credit

Package Includes: *Living Fossils, Living Fossils Teacher Guide, Living Fossils DVD; Parent Lesson Planner*

3 Book, 1 DVD Package
978-0-89051-763-5 $66.99

LIFE SCIENCE ORIGINS & SCIENTIFIC THEORY

1 year
10th – 12th grade
1 Credit

Package Includes: *Evolution: the Grand Experiment, Teacher Guide, DVD; Living Fossils, Teacher Guide, DVD; Parent Lesson Planner*

5 Book, 2 DVD Package
978-0-89051-761-1 $144.99

NATURAL SCIENCE THE STORY OF ORIGINS

1 year
10th – 12th grade
½ Credit

Package Includes: *Evolution: the Grand Experiment; Evolution: the Grand Experiment Teacher's Guide; Evolution: the Grand Experiment DVD; Parent Lesson Planner*

3 Book, 1 DVD Package
978-0-89051-762-8 $71.99

ADVANCED PRE-MED STUDIES

1 year
10th – 12th grade
1 Credit

Package Includes: *Building Blocks in Life Science; The Genesis of Germs; Body by Design; Exploring the History of Medicine; Parent Lesson Planner*

5 Book Package
978-0-89051-767-3 $76.99

BIBLICAL ARCHAEOLOGY

1 year
10th – 12th grade
1 Credit

Package Includes: *Unwrapping the Pharaohs; Unveiling the Kings of Israel; The Archaeology Book; Parent Lesson Planner.*

4 Book Package
978-0-89051-768-0 $99.99

CHRISTIAN HERITAGE

1 year
10th – 12th grade
1 Credit

Package Includes: *For You They Signed; Lesson Parent Planner*

2 Book Package
978-0-89051-769-7 $50.99

SCIENCE STARTERS: ELEMENTARY GENERAL SCIENCE & ASTRONOMY

1 year
3rd – 8th grade

Package Includes: *Water & Weather – Student, Student Journal, and Teacher; The Universe – Student, Teacher, & Student Journal; Parent Lesson Planner*

7 Book Package
978-0-89051-816-8 $54.99

ELEMENTARY WORLD HISTORY

1 year
5th – 8th

Package Includes: *The Big Book of History; Noah's Ark: Thinking Outside the Box (book and DVD); & Parent Lesson Planner*

3 Book, 1 DVD Package
978-0-89051-815-1 $66.96

ELEMENTARY GEOGRAPHY AND CULTURES

1 year
3rd – 6th grade

Package Includes: *Children's Atlas of God's World, Passport to the World, & Parent Lesson Planner*

3 Book Package
978-0-89051-814-4 $49.99

APPLIED SCIENCE: STUDIES OF GOD'S DESIGN IN NATURE

1 year
7th – 9th grade
1 Credit

Package Includes: *Made in Heaven, Champions of Invention, Discovery of Design, & Parent Lesson Planner*

4 Book Package
978-0-89051-812-0 $50.99

CONCEPTS OF BIOGEOLOGY & ASTRONOMY

1 year
7th – 9th grade
½ Credit

Package Includes: *Exploring the World Around You, Exploring the World of Astronomy, & Parent Lesson Planner*

3 Book Package
978-0-89051-813-7 $41.99

INTRO TO BIBLICAL GREEK

½ year language studies
7th – 12th
½ Credit

Package Includes: *It's Not Greek to Me DVD & Parent Lesson Planner*

1 Book, 1 DVD Package
978-0-89051-818-2 $33.99

INTRO TO ECONOMICS: MONEY, HISTORY, & FISCAL FAITH

½ year economics
9th – 12th
½ Credit

Package Includes: *Bankruptcy of Our Nation, Money Wise DVD, & Parent Lesson Planner*

2 Book, 4 DVD Package
978-0-89051-811-3 $57.99

Master Books®

P.O. Box 726
Green Forest, AR 72638

Visit masterbooks.net for additional information, look insides, video trailers, and more!